"MAKE NO LITTLE PLANS, THEY HAVE NO MAGIC TO STIR MEN'S BLOOD...."

DANIEL H. BURNHAM
ARCHITECT OF UNION STATION, 1909

# UNION STATION

A HISTORY OF WASHINGTON'S GRAND TERMINAL

CAROL M. HIGHSMITH AND TED LANDPHAIR

FEATURING PHOTOGRAPHS BY CAROL M. HIGHSMITH

UNION STATION VENTURE, WASHINGTON, D.C.

Union Station Venture
40 Massachusetts Avenue, N.E.
Washington, D.C. 20002

Produced by
Archetype Press, Washington, D.C.
Diane Maddex, Project Director
John Hovanec and Gretchen Smith Mui,
    Editorial Assistants
Robert L. Wiser, Designer

Printed in Singapore
10    9    8    7    6    5    4    3    2    1

Endleaves: An early photograph of the waiting room,
looking toward the West Hall and showing the
original mahogany benches, which were equipped
with steam heaters.

Page 1: Union Station's new train board, welcoming
travelers to the restored landmark.

Page 2: Louis Saint-Gaudens's stone sentinels over-
looking the Main Hall about 1914. Their shields were
added for modesty's sake.

Page 3: A central kiosk for dining in the Main Hall,
built during the 1980s renovation.

Page 4: The old Presidential Suite at the
terminal's east end, where dignitaries and royalty
were greeted.

Page 5: Restaurant seating in the former presidential
reception room, a use reserved for this elegant space
since Union Station reopened in 1988.

Page 6: The station's old Savarin Restaurant, where
well-heeled Washingtonians ate whether or not they
were traveling. Even train passengers had plenty
of time for a leisurely meal or a dozen oysters at the
popular raw bar.

Page 7: A shopping arcade occupying the former
Savarin space in the East Hall. It retains the opulence
of the old white-tablecloth restaurant.

Page 8: The Columbus Plaza fountain about 1926.
Some of the urchins who used to splash here went
on to work for the Washington Terminal Company
in the roundhouses and coach yards.

Page 9: Lorado Taft's statue of Christopher Columbus
on the fountain, dedicated in 1912.

Pages 10–11: The station's granite facade, with three
flagpoles representing Columbus's three ships.

Pages 16–17: Gilded column capitals supporting a
decorative entablature in the East Hall, once home to
the Savarin Restaurant.

Pages 32–33: Octagonal coffers in the Main Hall
ceiling, gilded since the restoration to catch the light
and reflect the station's monumentality.

Pages 52–53: Three pairs of allegorical sculptures on
the central portico by Louis Saint-Gaudens representing fire and electricity, freedom and imagination,
and agriculture and mechanics, endeavors reinforced
by inscriptions between them. Columbus guiding his
ship greets travelers at ground level.

Pages 68–69: A cast-iron column on one of the train
platforms, which in 1907 sheltered passengers on the
steam trains that first rolled into the station.

Pages 88–89: Holiday wreaths, inviting travelers,
shoppers, and visitors to enjoy the station's new life.

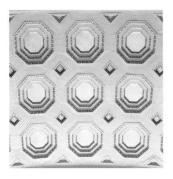

# C O N T E N T S

During the restoration of Union Station in the 1980s, the horologist Elton Howe got the old Main Hall clock ticking again. Although the roman numeral *IIII* may look odd, it was both faithful to Daniel Burnham's original and standard until well into the twentieth century. So was *VIIII* for *IX*. The yellow line arcing across the clock face is not a crack or an imperfection—it is a reflection of gold leaf glinting from the ceiling above.

IF, ON FEBRUARY 28, 1903, AS HE SIGNED "AN ACT to provide for a union station in the District of Columbia, and for other purposes," President Theodore Roosevelt could have known what "other purposes" the station would entertain one day, he might at least have sighed before signing. If the turn-of-the-century politicians who made Union Station the keystone of their plan to beautify Washington had divined that Orville and Wilbur Wright would achieve powered flight ten months later— and had they known what that wobbly flight would ultimately mean to train travel—they might have scaled back their rhetoric if not their blueprints.

But the railroads were king in 1903, so they commissioned an imperial transportation palace. From its grandeur to its decline and now to its renaissance, this is Union Station's story. The photographer Carol M. Highsmith spent parts of five years documenting the fall and the painstaking rise of this titanic building in the 1980s. She returned ten years after it reopened in 1988 to record its dramatic transformation into a vibrant crossroads for residents and visitors alike. Memorable and historic photographs came from other collections to complete a portrait of one of America's most significant landmarks. As the long life of this historic building unfolds in these pages, *Union Station: A History of Washington's Grand Terminal* brings back another era and helps keep vivid memories alive.

15

PART ONE

RENAISSANCE

# NEW LIFE FOR AN OLD STATION

NOT EVEN THE MOST COCKEYED OF OPTIMISTS WHO GAZED IN WONDER AT THE GLORIOUSLY RENOVATED UNION STATION IN 1988 COULD HAVE FORESEEN THE TRIUMPH THAT LAY AHEAD. IT WAS ONE THING TO WAX NOSTALGIC, TO COMMUNE WITH HAPPY GHOSTS IN THIS GREAT BEAUX ARTS LANDMARK, AND QUITE ANOTHER TO EMBRACE THE GALLERY OF SHOPS, KIOSKS, RESTAURANTS, AND FOOD BOOTHS. EMBRACE IT, WASHINGTON AND ITS VISITORS DID. AS THIS QUINTESSENTIAL MIXED-USE FACILITY MARKED ITS FIRST DECADE, SEVENTY THOUSAND PEOPLE A DAY WERE PASSING THROUGH, RETAIL SALES HAD EXCEEDED $100 MILLION A YEAR, AND THE FINANCIAL RETURN PER SQUARE FOOT RANKED SECOND AMONG AREA SHOPPING FACILITIES.

Designed to conjure up Christopher Columbus's days of discovery, a delicate figurehead by Lorado Taft projects from the ship's prow at the base of the marble fountain in Columbus Plaza (above). Four hundred years after his arrival, the explorer was much on the mind of the nation when Union Station was first conceived. The 1912 Columbus Fountain (opposite) depicts the Old and New Worlds and, under a globe, the indomitable Italian who brought the two together.

18

Railroads linked America shore to shore in the nineteenth century, and the symbolic importance of this fact was not lost on the planners of Union Station. Six allegorical sculptures by Louis Saint-Gaudens stand eighteen feet high above Ionic columns along the station's central portico (opposite). They represent fire (Prometheus), electricity (Thales) (right), freedom (Themis), imagination (Apollo), agriculture (Ceres), and mechanics (Archimedes)—pursuits that built America. Inscriptions for the ensemble, called *The Progress of Railroading*, were chosen by Charles W. Eliot, the president of Harvard, to underscore the cultural contributions of railroads to modern American life.

21

Alfresco diners (above) can now enjoy Union Station's grandeur outside as well as in. Looking east down the front arcade's series of groin vaults (opposite), one can further appreciate the timelessness of Daniel Burnham's classical design. In front of the Main Hall's towering arched skylight (pages 24–25), stone sentinels watch over travelers and tourists.

As the new millennium approached, resuscitated train stations were the rage across America. From the little depot in Pendleton, Oregon, to New York City's historic Grand Central Terminal, stations were reawakening as museums, shopping arcades, and even hotels. But none could match the appeal of Washington's Union Station. In a decade the terminal became the hub of Amtrak's revitalized Northeast Corridor operations—and its corporate headquarters—and it also captured the affection of local Metro train riders, Capitol Hill residents, congressional members and staffs, tourists from the world over, shoppers of all ages and races, history lovers and train buffs, moviegoers, restaurant patrons, commuters from as far away as Baltimore and Fredericksburg, Virginia, and folks looking for a quick souvenir or bite to eat in the food court. So successful was the venture that LaSalle Partners, which manages the fashion and gift stores and restaurants, was asked to take over other such projects in New York City, Chicago, Kansas City, and smaller markets.

"We *don't* use Washington's Union Station as an example of restoration and reuse," said Brian O'Connell, vice president for development of the Great American Station Foundation, the nonprofit organization that promotes the preservation and transformation of railroad stations nationwide. "Union Station has too much going for it. It would be unrealistic for others to match this kind of success."

The Great Train Store (opposite) is probably the most appropriate tenant in the new station marketplace. All the services train passengers may need—ticketing, baggage checking, and snacks to carry on board—can be found along the Concourse (right). One of the original platform gates now leads to a waiting area.

Not only trains of all descriptions come and go from Union Station. So do automobiles, buses and taxis, local and long-distance tour buses, and even amphibious tour boats, bound for a splash in the Potomac. As the once-dogeared Capitol Hill neighborhood has rebounded with new office buildings, museums, hotels, and congressional and U.S. Supreme Court facilities, foot traffic has far outpaced expectations. Unlike a typical mall, Union Station has become a rendezvous spot—*the most-visited destination in the nation's capital.* Venerable Union Station has evolved into *the* place to catch a movie or meal; enjoy a holiday display, an art exhibit, or an international festival; shop at a unique—usually nonchain—store or booth; or soak up Daniel Burnham's architectural splendor at a private party, inaugural ball, embassy reception, or corporate gala for fifty—or ten thousand—guests. In 1998, when the station gained control of air rights over the tracks behind the terminal, plans began to take shape for even more ambitious development to usher this storied national landmark into its second century.

At the entrance to
the station's East Hall,
a magnificent semi-
circular window invites
light in, silhouetting the
roman numeral clock
and a row of the forty-
six soldiers sculpted
by Louis Saint-Gaudens
(above and right).
Properly placing the
soldiers historically was
once a Washington
cottage industry. They
most closely resemble
second-century war-
riors from Gaul, who
served as mercenaries
in the Roman army.

Looking toward the West Hall (opposite), Daniel Burnham's passion for natural light is obvious. Sunbeams stream through the arched skylight in what was originally Union Station's ticketing and baggage-checking area. Today diners can climb closer to the monumental ceiling to take in the architectural panorama.

Tucked into an alcove of the old Presidential Suite at the far end of the East Hall, now a restaurant, an eagle shield ringed in silver (right) kept a vigil over important guests visiting the station. During the restoration, artisans recreated the East Hall's decorative frieze (below).

# HUFFING TOWARD THE CITY BEAUTIFUL

IN 1800 AMERICA'S NEW CAPITAL WAS A HORSE-AND-MULE TOWN. STAGECOACHES CARRIED A HUNDRED PASSENGERS A DAY, AT MOST, FROM WILLARD'S AND BROWN'S HOTELS THROUGH THE WOODS NORTH OF MASSACHUSETTS AVENUE TO THE MARYLAND TOWN OF BLADENSBURG, AND THEN ON TO BALTIMORE. EVEN AS THE BALTIMORE & OHIO RAILROAD BEGAN TO THRUST WESTWARD FROM MARYLAND'S BIG PORT CITY IN 1828, SEDENTARY WASHINGTON WAS PINNING ITS HOPES ON WATER TRANSIT: PACKET BOATS UP THE PO-TOMAC AND BARGES ON THE FETID CITY CANAL AND THE NEW CHESAPEAKE & OHIO CANAL TO THE WEST.

When Currier and Ives made a color print of Washington in 1880 (opposite), train tracks crossed both Pennsylvania Avenue and the Mall. The noise, the dirt, and the unsightliness of it all eventually nudged officials to build a new gateway to the nation's capital—a majestic union station.

An 1864 B&O placard (right) promised "speed, security and comfort," important considerations for Civil War–era travelers worried about Confederate acts of sabotage. Thanks to the Union Army, passengers no longer had to transfer in Alexandria.

But when the Maryland General Assembly authorized a B&O line to Bladensburg, shrewdly higgling a twenty percent cut of passenger revenues for its troubles, Washington could no longer keep the railroad out; Congress approved an extension to a makeshift depot in an old tailor's shop on Pennsylvania Avenue, a locomotive plume's distance from the Capitol. In 1835 about eight hundred citizens gathered to greet the B&O trains, pulled by twelve-horsepower steam engines aptly christened the Washington, Adams, Jefferson, and Madison.

The B&O kept Baltimore time, several minutes off Washington's reckoning by the sun, and capital locals who consulted their timepieces risked missing their trains. Helpfully, a giant bell hallooed each departure. It was one of many annoyances to the depot's neighbor, Congress, which soon introduced a bill declaring the place "a nuisance, where the idle gathered." Departures swelled to six a day, so freight business was booming, and the line had outgrown what an observer called its "filthy" rowhouse depot. The B&O in 1858 thus moved a few blocks northeast to an elaborate new Italianate building modeled after the railroad's Baltimore terminal. The station on Pennsylvania Avenue quickly became a tavern.

Switching sites did little to quell the railroad's racket in the halls of Congress, especially after the B&O stretched a spur across Pennsylvania Avenue through the Capitol's shadow, in hopes of connecting with southern lines at the Long Bridge on the Potomac. It took the Union Army to forge the link in 1861; until then, passengers had to tote their valises or jangle across the bridge in omnibuses to catch the Alexandria & Washington, a humble, six-mile line that connected with the Orange & Alexandria Railroad to the south. During the Civil War, the Union Army moved throngs of soldiers south by rail across the Long Bridge into battle. In 1868 a writer perched on Capitol Hill would still find that "shrill screams of the engine[s would] frequently interfere with debate."

Washington's first depot on Pennsylvania Avenue (above) was hardly imposing. The B&O parked its steam engines and open cars behind this converted tailor's shop in 1835 and, sometime after this sketch was rendered, erected a belfry with which to peal arrivals and departures. Early trains crossed city streets at grade, spooking dray horses and menacing human life and limb. For a time, capital commissioners required the iron horses to stop at the city line and be drawn slowly by horses into the Pennsylvania Avenue station.

An 1839 view showed one of the first train routes alongside Tiber Creek (opposite top), so named to recall the grandeur that was Rome. Tiber Creek then looked like a rustic brook refreshing the "Swampoodle" slum, but by 1850 (opposite bottom) the area had degenerated into an "indescribable cesspool" full of "smells and malarial mosquitos." By 1907 both were mere memories, as they were filled in and paved over for Union Station and its train yards.

36

1889.     Tiber creek.

North east of the Capitol          Washington

At the Capitol's west gate about 1866 (left), a Washington & Georgetown Company horse-drawn streetcar was loaded, and an Alexandria & Washington steam locomotive paused to allow notables to pass. The wide smokestack was to catch burning embers.

As the Seventy-first Regiment arrived in 1861, it was hard to believe that the second B&O depot (top) sat two blocks from the Capitol. Civil War Washington was a sea of blue and a cloud of dust from all the marching feet.

The B&O tower sank into a landfilled bowl (above), and patrons descended ramps and stairs to the track level. Train cars were wooden with open vestibules—passengers had to contend with a snootful of locomotive smoke.

On July 2, 1881, President James A. Garfield was heading out of town from the Pennsy's Baltimore & Potomac station for a seaside break in New Jersey. Charles J. Guiteau lunged and landed a mortal shot (above). Garfield died about ten weeks later. The railroad marked the spot with a star. The Pennsy's brooding station, train sheds, and tracks (left) compounded the cluttered jumble on the Mall—far from the open grounds of today.

Awakened to the money to be made from a route into Washington, the B&O's archrival, the Pennsylvania Railroad, completed an end run, buying the rights to an obscure and dormant line, the Baltimore & Potomac, that serviced the tobacco towns of southern Maryland. Crafty Pennsy agents had spotted a loophole in the railroad's charter that permitted construction of a spur up to twenty miles long anywhere on the main line. So the Pennsylvania set about snaking just such a branch from the town of Bowie in Maryland, across the Anacostia River, past the Washington Navy Yard, along "Dead Man's Curve" on Virginia Avenue, and into a new terminal. For that depot and train yard, Congress helpfully granted the new B&P fourteen acres of public land on the Mall, close to the city's sprawling Center Market.

The B&P station would earn a black mark for more than cinders and soot. In 1881 President James A. Garfield was shot there by a demented office seeker; a star on the floor marked the spot. During a particularly relentless spring flood in 1889, the terminal's night matron, Alberta Shaughnessy (honored for her sharp eye in spotting "suspicious characters" like "Chicago Mae," a notorious diamond thief), was observed rowing a boat across the depot's waiting room, scooping up carp.

B&O trains across the "Avenue of the Presidents" were bad enough. The clutter of Pennsy tracks, train sheds, and huffing steam engines on what was supposed to be Pierre L'Enfant's sylvan Mall proved maddening. Twenty-seven evergreens planted along a ring of dirt that had been built as a sort of station blind had to be moved when it was discovered that locomotive smoke was killing them. So voracious were the railroads that the *Washington Star* suggested the Capitol itself as an ideal roundhouse. "In ten years' time," despaired one U.S. senator, "there will not be a rod square of ground in all the Government reservations that is not occupied by a railroad depot with all its dirty surroundings."

In 1901, a year after toasting Washington's centennial with odes to its future as a City Beautiful, a Senate commission charged with improving parks had had enough of raucous terminals, deadly grade crossings, and belching locomotives. It ordered the railroads away from the Mall—the B&O north, the Pennsy south. But the monumental dreams of one of the nation's master architects and the clout of a captain of railroading would soon trump that directive.

Early passenger coupon books and timetables (above) were sometimes ornate and served to promote the line's service; many have become collectors' treasures. This design enhanced a Pennsylvania Railroad Boston-to-Washington route guide and timetable.

Trains and streetcars and their tracks all changed the character of the Mall and the Capitol grounds, as *Harper's Weekly* illustrated on March 7, 1895, in *Winter at the National Capitol* (opposite), drawn by Charles Graham. Trolleys ran down Pennsylvania Avenue to Center Market (left), seen about 1900 not far from the Pennsylvania Railroad's Baltimore & Potomac terminal.

After marching from the D.C. Armory near Center Market to a B&P freight platform at Ninth Street and Maryland Avenue, S.W. (above), First D.C. Regiment infantry volunteers left May 14, 1898, on a special Southern Railway train to mobilize for the Spanish-American War. The *Star* reported that mothers and sisters, "to say nothing of sweethearts," gave the soldiers a rousing sendoff.

A T THE TURN OF THE CENTURY DANIEL H. BURN-
HAM LOOKED, TRAVELED, AND DAYDREAMED
ALIKE THE PROSPEROUS WORLD ARCHITECT
HE WAS. MASTER OF THE EPIC WORLD'S COLUMBIAN
EXPOSITION IN CHICAGO IN 1893, HE HAD HELPED
UNCORK AN AMERICAN WELLSPRING OF BEAUX ARTS
FERVOR. AS ARCHITECT OF THE REGAL PENNSYLVANIA
RAILROAD, BURNHAM HAD ALREADY CHALKED UP A
NEW PENNSYLVANIA STATION IN PITTSBURGH BY THE
TIME HE WAS INVITED TO ORCHESTRATE A SWEEPING
CITY BEAUTIFUL PLAN FOR WASHINGTON, DESIGNED
TO OUTFIT IT IN A COLOSSAL MANNER BEFITTING A
STRIPLING WORLD CAPITAL. THE CITY LACKED A MEMO-
RIAL TO ABRAHAM LINCOLN, SUFFICIENT EXECUTIVE
BRANCH OFFICES WITHIN HAILING DISTANCE OF THE
WHITE HOUSE, A BRIDGE FROM VIRGINIA TO L'ENFANT'S
ELM-LINED MALL, AND ESPECIALLY A PLAN TO RID THE
MALL OF ITS TAWDRY BUILDINGS AND TRAIN TRACKS.

44

America's master archi-
tect Daniel H. Burnham
(above) finally gave the
city a fitting railroad
terminal. Union Station
took its place as the
first piece in the whole-
sale transformation
of Washington from a
swampy backwater
town into a monumental
world capital.

The station's final grand
plaza scheme (opposite
top) ended up being
somewhat more modest
than the fanciful visions
(center and bottom)
that were inspired
by the 1893 World's
Columbian Exposition,
which saluted Chris-
topher Columbus's
voyage to America. This
aggrandized series of
peristyles, reminiscent
of the Place de la Con-
corde in Paris, was
intended to pay proper
homage to the Capitol.
Neither the tight-fisted
railroads nor Congress
would pay for such
extravagance, however.

Burnham promptly set off with other members of the United States Senate Park Commission (known as the McMillan Commission of 1901–2)—colleagues all, from the Chicago world's fair—on a regal tour of European capitals. At the Piazza de Republicca two blocks from the Rome train station, he scribbled sketches of the Baths of Diocletian, the royal gym that had once featured (slave-driven) forced-air heat. Burnham's "Make no little plans" credo would become architectural legend.

While the commissioners were off jaunting, the Pennsylvania Railroad was muscling control of the B&O. When Burnham ran into the line's president, Alexander Cassatt, in London, he asked him, Why not build a single "union station" that would give Washington back its unspoiled vistas, project the Pennsylvania's newfound hubris, and set the tone for the whole Washington plan? In return for a federal payment of $3 million to offset construction costs of a tunnel under Capitol Hill needed to connect with southern lines, Cassatt agreed.

Burnham's barrel-vaulted terminal would rise above the sewery remnants of Tiber Creek, on the edge of "Swampoodle," an infamous Irish shantytown. In *Mr. Lincoln's City,* Richard M. Lee wrote that the area had once been notorious for its "dirtiness, crime and dubious loyalty to the Union . . . the ideal place to turn a dishonest dollar." Residents kept goats amid decrepit buildings and the B&O coal yards. To construct his own Diocletian edifice beginning in October 1903, Burnham brought in Italian labor gangs and lodged them in camp cars. The laborers patronized Irish stores and St. Aloysius Church but fought regularly with their neighbors.

Before a single stone was in place, the workers spent a year building up the street grade and pouring concrete footings into the swampy soil. Across the site they spread close to four million cubic yards of fill dirt, enough to pack eighty thousand hoppers stretching six hundred miles. Gradually a bog twenty feet above mean tide was elevated to what *Building News* in 1908 called "an area of eminence" sixty feet above tide level over many acres. Taking together the construction of a massive terminal, plaza, tunnel under the Library of Congress, and train yard complex and removal from the Washington cityscape of two sprawling railroad eyesores, the Union Station project was herculean. Observed Robert Vogel, a former curator of the Smithsonian Institution's Division of Engineering and Industry, "It was a whole lot more than the mere construction of a building where none had been."

47

Although construction began in 1903, the first granite slabs did not rise until 1905, and by January 1907 (opposite top) the Concourse and Main Hall were just beginning to emerge. Underneath it all was a modern steel frame. Union Station fit comfortably into District life by the 1920s (bottom). As one participant, the architect Edward H. Bennett, saw the City Beautiful movement, "To make our city loved, we must make it lovely."

It is not hard to understand why McNulty Brothers rigged up a well-braced "moving scaffold," or "traveler," to complete the grueling construction of and delicate finishing work on Union Station's Main Hall ceiling from 1905 to 1907 (above). Imagine the alternative: having to tear down and rebuild the scaffolding to reach each section along more than 220 feet of Roman barrel-vaulted ceiling, ninety feet high. The same moving scaffold technique was used eight decades later for the restoration.

Camera shutter speeds were slow in 1908, a year after Union Station opened, when a photographer caught this view of the Concourse (above). It was a good thing that passengers spent little time here, for it was unheated and uncooled. Lighting also proved a difficult challenge. The skylight cast cheery light by day, but at night lights trained on the ceiling washed out any distinction between glasswork and ornamental plaster.

The first slab of white Vermont granite was laid at the northeast corner of the station site in 1905. Architects, engineers, and inspectors dropped coins onto the mortar, where, the *Star* reported, they "will find an abiding place for many years to come." But the granite megaliths were strictly ornamental. A steel frame, encased in concrete for fire protection, bore the building's massive load. Into Union Station, Burnham built a central vacuum cleaning system; crude cooling fans that blew air across revolving, brine-soaked burlap sheets; and a system of clocks synchronized from a master clock in the third-floor telegraph office. So immense were the new station's waiting room and Concourse that a critic snorted, "Spring meets you at the train, and by the time you walk through to the exit, winter has come upon you."

The effect was properly pompous: Constantinian arches, egg-and-dart molding and sun-streaked gilt leafing, coffered ceilings and majestic skylights, delicate Pompeian traceries, towering statues inside and out by Louis Saint-Gaudens, the less-famous brother of Augustus Saint-Gaudens. The six twenty-five-ton figures outside symbolize, on the ends, fire and electricity, agriculture and mechanics, and, between them, freedom and imagination. Inside, behind the stone soldiers looming high above the Main Hall, Burnham hid huge arc lights, trained upward to produce a natural-light effect against the eggshell-white plaster ceiling. His Concourse immediately became the world's largest hall; it was said to be spacious enough to hold America's standing army (then fifty thousand strong) or the Washington Monument laid flat. Construction of thirty-four platforms and sixty miles of track in the yards proceeded out back.

Union Station quickly became a landmark, immortalized on picture postcards (below). This one shows its new next-door neighbor, the U.S. Post Office, completed in 1915 by Burnham's successor firm to continue the Beaux Arts symmetry of the station complex. With its triple-arched center pavilion and flanking arcades, the terminal calls up the days of Rome and the triumphal arches that signified arrival at an important spot in the road.

Burnham designed rooms that over time would support a dining hall and soda fountain; a "room set aside for the exclusive use of invalids"; a Presidential Suite later filled with furnishings of red leather, "priceless" rugs, and crystal electroliers; a reading room; a social hall; a bowling alley; a billiard parlor; sleeping quarters; railroad offices; a tonsorial and shoeshine parlor; and even an upstairs space so long that the District of Columbia police department would rent it as a pistol range. The station featured not only "large and commodious" men's and women's restrooms but also vast lounges for each sex. The men's anteroom became a smoking parlor, complete with the second-largest cigar stand in town.

Burnham commissioned the president of Harvard University, Charles W. Eliot, to pick the inscriptions for the outdoor pavilions; Eliot would write several himself. The most familiar, because it is etched above the west carriage way—the only entrance most passengers would eventually be permitted to use—was a quote from Samuel Johnson:

> HE THAT WOULD BRING HOME THE
> WEALTH OF THE INDIES MUST CARRY
> THE WEALTH OF THE INDIES WITH HIM
> SO IT IS IN TRAVELLING—A MAN
> MUST CARRY KNOWLEDGE WITH HIM
> IF HE WOULD BRING HOME KNOWLEDGE

Eliot took it upon himself to comment on Saint-Gaudens's sculptures. "The necks all seem to me long in proportion to the length of the face, particularly Freedom's neck." Burnham soothed him by noting that long necks are essential to statuary that is viewed from ninety feet below.

49

New Post Office and Union Station, Washington, D. C.

A student from Pomona College in Claremont, California, Helmus Andrews, was asked by Saint-Gaudens to model for the interior legionnaires. Forty-seven years later, Andrews would visit the station for the first time. He pronounced the forty-six final products "pretty crummy." If Eliot's criticisms of Saint-Gaudens's stonework could be ignored, those of the terminal's board of directors could not. "In blushing deference" to their female passengers—lest they take offense at the scantily attired soldiers, some of whom wore thigh-length tunic skirts and others nothing but a cape down their backsides—Saint-Gaudens was ordered to provide shields as modesty panels. Perhaps he protested that no more than a nebulous bump betrayed the guards' stony masculinity, but he complied.

True to the legacy of the Columbian Exposition, Burnham's plans called for a majestic plaza, ringed by peristyles and falling toward Pennsylvania Avenue along a new, diagonal avenue. As Louisiana Avenue, the street would be built and lined with trees in the 1930s, but its sweeping rows of columns got no further than the drafting board. In 1912 the plaza did receive a fountain featuring Lorado Taft's heroic sculpture of Christopher Columbus and depicting themes of the Old and New Worlds, one as an old man, the other an Indian. The opening ceremony drew thousands of Knights of Columbus from across America, riding more than a hundred special trains and jingling the cash registers of the Washington Terminal Company.

Another Burnham brainstorm—that the plaza would be an ideal home for Lincoln's memorial—died quickly. During World War I a writer would observe that the area between the station plaza and the Capitol, where "temporary" dormitories for female government workers were rising, "leads only to weedgrown fields."

At 2:52 A.M. on Sunday, October 27, 1907, the last train left the old B&O terminal, bound for Pittsburgh. Union Station's first train, from Pittsburgh, arrived the same morning at 6:50. Excitement abounded when B&O and Pennsylvania trains entered the yard together for the first time on November 17. For the station's formal opening almost a year later, veteran railroad employee H. P. Baldwin was permitted to buy the first ticket. It was photographed and, a newspaper reported, presented to "Miss Kathryn Purnell, an Actress," who went to Baltimore.

Wartime—when hale men were off at the front and women by the thousands filled civilian government jobs—was a recent memory in this photograph from about 1922. Female defense workers bunked in these hastily built "tempos" between the Capitol and Union Station where baseball diamonds had once sprawled. The first Senate office building, now named the Richard B. Russell Building, is on the right.

WASHINGTON WAS PROPERLY IMPRESSED BY ITS MIGHTY "GRAND VESTIBULE." AS *THE WASHINGTON SKETCH BOOK* NOTED IN 1935, "A TRAVELLER, ARRIVING BY TRAIN AND PASSING THROUGH GATES TO A [CONCOURSE] LONGER AND BROADER THAN THE CAPITOL OF THE UNITED STATES, FEELS VERY STRANGE AND INSIGNIFICANT. AND IMMEDIATELY GETS A PROPER ATTITUDE TOWARD THE IMPORTANCE OF WASHINGTON." EVEN THE STATION'S MAHOGANY BENCHES DREW THE WRITER'S ADMIRATION. "THEY COULD BE NO SOFTER IF THEY HAD CUSHIONS, SUCH IS THEIR GENERAL COMFORT. IT WOULD TAKE A POET TO SING THE WORTH OF THESE BENCHES."

55

Eleanor Roosevelt waited to be presented by her husband, Franklin, to Queen Elizabeth at a June 8, 1939, reception in the Presidential Suite (opposite). George VI was next in line, although only his epaulets show. Behind the president was his secretary, General E. M. Watson, and farther up were Mrs. Cordell Hull and her husband, the secretary of state.

By the 1960s only holidays produced much of a rush at Union Station. One lad (left) caught forty winks on a Concourse bench on July 5, 1962. Arrival and departure times were changed electrically, but other information was adjusted by a gateman, using a long pole like the ones used to move classroom windows.

The terminal's Savarin Restaurant, named for a fabled nineteenth-century French gourmand, served city eminents as well as train travelers. "Anybody who was anybody dined there," recalled Albert W. Browne in 1988. He had worked as a Pullman porter in the 1920s. "Remember, people were traveling long distances; they wanted a fine dinner before they left." Because Union Station was the juncture between North and South and among seven passenger lines, customers had time to loll between connections, browsing through any of seven daily Washington newspapers. "The restaurant, the men's smoker, the whole atmosphere was refined, for the elite traveler," Browne remembered. "Why, the barber shop had twelve chairs and a boot-black and a valet to press your clothes." Ironically, the former presidential adviser Charles A. Horsky recalled that the Savarin was "the only nice place in Washington you could dine with a black man."

The terminal was a magnet for the masses as well. "It was hot, plenty hot, in Washington in the summertime," said Browne. "But Union Station had those high ceilings. People would go inside just to cool off. It was a case of survival of the fittest!" Others remembered splashing, with an eye peeled for the terminal detective, in the Columbus Plaza fountain.

So crowded was the station in 1945 that Red Cap James "Doc" Carter would recollect thirty-five years later, "People used to bribe me to put them in wheelchairs so they could get to the trains in front of the crowds." During World War II the army sergeant George Timko, who had already been wounded in Germany, suffered a broken leg when he was trampled by a holiday crowd. E. L. Thompson, a writer, observed, "The depot looks more like an army camp than a railroad station." In the USO lounge, the hostess Anna Adams was moved to proclaim Union Station "the crossroad of the world." The terminal added a window to each ticket bay and built "coach only" and "Pullman only" ticket booths in the middle of the floor. Out back, platforms had to be lengthened to handle longer trains.

East and west porte cocheres at the station were among the first designed for automobiles rather than horse-drawn phaetons. In the 1920s tussles over a taxicab (above) were common, as overnight sleepers emptied hundreds of travelers at a time. Washington residents, who have long lived with a taxicab zone system, will recognize an anachronism on this cab: a meter. In fact, this vehicle was known as a "taximeter cabriolet."

Travelers waited for their trains on benches under the Main Hall's barrel-vaulted ceiling (above), an impressive space modeled after the Baths of Diocletian in Rome. Columns screened the ticketing and baggage area to the west and the dining room to the east. For those who did not have the time or the cash to dine at the elegant Savarin Restaurant in the East Hall, Union Station's soda fountain (left) was a by-no-means-plain alternative.

The *Washington Post* found "girl broadcasters" replacing time-honored male train callers gone off to war, the women's "sweet voices having special appeal" to servicemen. No longer, reported the paper, "does one see a leather-lunged train caller raise a battered megaphone to the general vicinity of his mouth and hear him voice the old familiar bellow: 'Train leaving on track 26 for Bal'more, P'burgh, Youngsto'n, Clevean', Dayton, Ind'nap'luss, Chiccago and all points westtt.'" The *Post* was flashing its poetic license, as track 26 served long-haul trains to the Carolinas and points south. Women wearing slacks, low-heeled shoes, and "free and easy" clothing went to work cleaning coaches and even repairing 1,000-horsepower switching locomotives. They were taught two safety rules: "Don't stand on a rail, and don't stand in the middle of a track."

World War II, wrote Haynes Johnson in his 1980s novel *The Landing*, had transformed Union Station into "a pulsing nerve center . . . something more than a railroad station; now it, and the people who streamed through it, were part of an endless procession linked, inextricably, somehow, to the great release of raw energy that had been set in motion across the American continent." Arriving passengers faced a battle royal hailing a taxi. "Unaggressive people have been known to wait for an hour," wrote one onlooker. Diamond Cab's concession was described by the hackers' association president as "the most expensive in the world."

Even in its later dotage, the terminal would feel isolated surges of life: crusty railroad workers watched celebrants at the christening of the B&O's new streamliner, the Cincinnatian, in 1947 "spill martinis down her sleek, blue sides." In 1963 more than twenty special trains, each carrying a thousand people, streamed into Washington for the August civil rights march. Arriving passengers filled the Concourse with freedom songs; hundreds more would-be marchers were left behind for lack of room on trains.

During the height of World War II, information clerks answered eighty thousand questions a day from the one hundred thousand persons who passed through the terminal (opposite). Just before Christmas in 1942, crowds got so thick that passengers had difficulty finding the door; servicemen desperately jumped train gates in their rush to get home, and for parts of two days the management actually closed and locked the station to any more passengers.

Union Station was Washington's principal point of departure for soldiers and sailors heading off to basic training during World War II (above). The station's USO lounge affixed colored tags to sleeping servicemen so they could be awakened in time to catch their trains.

## HAUTE COUTURE AND THE HOI POLLOI

BEGGARS AND BEDOUIN PRINCES, RED CAPS AND RED MEN, MODEL RAILROADERS AND MEMBERS OF CONGRESS HAVE ALL MINGLED IN UNION STATION'S VAULTED ROOMS: LINDBERGH, PICKFORD, KHRUSHCHEV, CHURCHILL, AND MEMBERS OF THE COMMUNITY FOR CREATIVE NONVIOLENCE AMONG THEM.

Units of the army's First Division (left) passed through Washington in September 1919 en route from Germany, where they had fought and then served briefly as an army of occupation after Armistice Day. As regular army troops, they were on their way to peacetime assignments at posts across the country. At a late-summer repast at Union Station, the doughboys and their guests feasted on watermelon. In 1903 Teddy Roosevelt (opposite) signed the act that paved the way for the capital's grand terminal. After the station opened, the former Rough Rider stopped by and chatted with some of the men who kept the wheels rolling.

One day before World War I the baggage foreman George H. Thomas and his men turned the station inside out, looking for two missing pieces of luggage. "I found them in what has always seemed to me the tragic nick of time," he told the *Post* when he retired in 1953. "In another hour or two their owner would have had to postpone his sailing for Europe—aboard the *Lusitania*."

In 1936 the Main Hall was cleared so three thousand dignitaries from fifty-four nations could be fed at the World Power Conference. As a twenty-eight-piece orchestra serenaded from the balcony, guests consumed four hundred Virginia lambs, nine thousand select olives, a carload of broccoli, and forty-five hundred stalks of "choice celery placed at the right moment" before them. The *Star* marveled at "the delicate business of serving wines to foreign personages, and the delivery of ice cream before it melts away."

Ordinary folk became the stuff of anecdotes as well. In 1933 F. E. Prior observed overnight cleaning crews "swinging along the smooth floor as if to the rhythm wrung out of a suds wagon and played on nine-foot mop handles." Night after night this "ceremonial dance of the cleaners is repeated," he wrote. "A long follow-through and a relaxing swing as the long handle slips out its full length [and is] caught at the tip in the left hand while the scrubber's right foot is carried in a graceful arc over its mate." The crews' nemesis, another witching-hour visitor wrote, was chewing gum "firmly planted everywhere but in the wastebasket." The terminal's Lost and Found staff turned up umbrellas, army rifles, underwear, and false teeth. "Mr. Marshall, baggage master, hopes that some day women will learn not to park rings and teeth in washrooms."

Union Station's "ladies' retiring room" (below) featured fine tapestries and a smoke-free place to meet friends. The equivalent men's waiting room, or smoker, featured a cigar stand, bootblack, and barber shop. This women's facility would later get more furniture, including several rocking chairs, and an attendant who saw to the visitors' comfort.

It may not have been an uptown drawing room, but the poolroom at the station's YMCA, maintained for railroad workers on the third floor of the east wing, looked spiffy enough in 1920 (above). There was even a reading room in the back.

In 1934 the *Post* writer Robert Cruise McManus found, besides an "antlike army" of station workers, "thirty thousand bankers, Gypsies, immigrants, Aunt Minnies, Senators, salesmen, football fans and funeral goers." He caught a basketball game at the YMCA gymnasium "up there somewhere" and watched huge "perambulators" thunder past, carrying pea soup for the lunchroom. Someone interviewed a ticket taker, who reported the longest ticket sold to be a round-the-world voucher, paid for in cash.

Privileged visitors got a peek at the Metropolitan Southern Railroad, an elaborate model layout built in 1939 by area businessmen and enjoyed by off-duty train crews. Scenery depicted the landscape between Washington and Baltimore, "with a few western hills thrown in." To dispel any notion that their doings were kids' stuff or their creations toys, the rail club banned minors.

"Old cranks" remained a Red Cap's biggest headache, lamented the dean of Union Station porters, John D. Sellers. "Women of the old school in particular, like creatures out of Dickens," asking innumerable questions. Sellers reported tips as meager as fifteen cents by a Vanderbilt and as lavish as a dollar by an "average man." Henry Ford's tip, he added, was thirty-five cents.

When he was president, William Howard Taft (above) was so portly that he could not be comfortably seated in the Presidential Suite's modest wicker furnishings. Many years later, tens of pounds lighter, and recovering from a hospital stay, Taft, then the chief justice of the United States, was wheeled to his train for a Canadian getaway. Within a year, in February 1930, he was further incapacitated and forced to retire. On March 8, 1930, he died at the age of seventy-two.

On April 14, 1945, the coffin containing the body of President Franklin D. Roosevelt was transferred from the Conneaught (right), a private car on the funeral train from the Little White House in Georgia. Guards arranged the caisson in preparation for the slow procession to the White House. Railroads were expert at transporting the dead; entire morgue trains were a regular sight during wartime and influenza epidemics. Tradition called for a double fare: one for the corpse and one for the person accompanying the body.

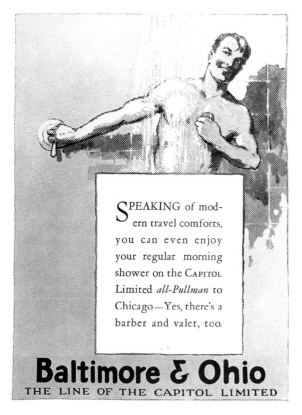
General Haile Selassie bowed to Jacqueline Kennedy as President John F. Kennedy waited to greet the Ethiopian emperor (opposite) in October 1963. Union Station was the Washington arrival point of many dignitaries, some of whom, like Morocco's King Hassan, rode in style in elaborate private cars.

To believe this promotional piece (above), the B&O's Capitol Limited had all the comforts of home. Competition was fierce between the B&O and Pennsy for the prime long-distance run, overnight to Chicago; the two railroads' premier trains west even left at the same time. Rival engineers would race each other out of the station, or at least appear to, to the delight of yard gangs.

Thousands of mourners huddled beneath the three flagpoles in front of the station in 1945, awaiting the return of Franklin Roosevelt's body from Warm Springs, Georgia. Workers once had scaled one of the poles to twist its gilded eagle to the right. Someone had complained that the eagle looked east, toward nondescript houses, rather than south, toward the source of inspiration and federal largesse—the Capitol.

President Truman stopped by in 1951 to once again turn the Presidential Suite into a USO "VIP" installation "for just about the most important people of all," the men and women of the armed services. Bess Truman followed, days later, to cut another ribbon for a "Little Lounge—for ladies." The facilities would revive a USO tradition: pinning colored labels to napping military personnel so wake-up calls would be on time.

Station operations superintendent Paul Dowell, who retired in 1978, reminisced about a woman's barging into his office, demanding to be escorted to her husband's train compartment. "She said she was going to kill him," Dowell told the *Star*, "and sure enough, she pulled a gun out of her purse." The railroad official mollified her by explaining that, once purchased, a man's compartment is his castle, and "what happens once you're inside is your own private business." Yet another retirement, by the "Mayor of Union Station," manager Bernard R. Tolson, brought its own story. "A guy who said he just got out of the pen in New England popped in one day and summed up his assets," he said. "A little change, a railroad ticket to Colorado, and some clothing. He needed some traveling money. I gave him a little and told him to forget it. He did."

There were other incidents: Two boxcars, loaded with beer, uncoupling from a train at Takoma Park, rolling backward toward the station; they smashed into a pillar and three parked coaches, and railroad crews labored through the night to slosh up the foamy debris. The 1961 walk-through of the station basement, its walls four feet thick—the cellar was intended by Burnham as a men's steam room and swimming pool, but this day it was eyed as a nuclear-fallout shelter. The 1978 sit-in by the homeless, who spread foam mats and lugged in pots of coffee and food; eventually locked out, they dispersed into a bitter-cold night's air.

Even days before it was to be boarded shut in 1981, Union Station hosted an inaugural "Taste of America." The *Post* food critic Phyllis Richman called it "a four-day snackathon" plied by thirty-seven restaurants. Amid the fallen plaster and oily carpet stains, one hundred thousand celebrants wolfed down snails, fresh prawns, and zucchini curry soup.

In 1942 the *Washington Times-Herald's* Helen Essary had watched crowds of soldiers: "romantic-eyed dreamers made into fighting men against their wishes." But as Essary gazed outside the station and skyward, she would write, presciently, "The Magic Carpet is now the airplane. It awaits anybody with imagination."

67

Maryland Department of Transportation

MARC

← Track 17
Location C

Track 18 →
**Location C**

# L  I  F  E     O  N     B  O  A  R  D

RAILROAD EXECUTIVES ARE A TACITURN LOT. SO IT IS HARDLY SURPRISING THAT BOUND MINUTES, SOME CRUMBLING, FROM SEVEN DECADES OF WASHINGTON TERMINAL COMPANY BOARD OF DIRECTORS' MEETINGS WOULD BE SPARSE AND STRICTLY BUSINESS. TRACK LAYOUTS WERE CHANGED, VENDOR LEASES NEGOTIATED, PENSIONS APPROVED, AND MATTERS SUCH AS "APPLYING POWER-OPERATED REVERSE GEAR TO W. T. ENGINES 27 AND 36" DEBATED. BUT TUCKED IN THE FADED MIMEOGRAPHY ARE FLEETING TRACES OF THE TERMINAL'S DAILY LIFE:

A pillar on each of Union Station's platforms contained signal boxes (above), with which train conductors communicated with K tower. An explanation from the 1908 *Book of the Royal Blue:* "About a minute before the train is ready to leave the station the conductor signals that fact to the tower . . . by placing a key in one of the signal boxes." At the appointed time, another turn of the key signaled to all concerned that the train was ready to proceed. The coaches were from the B&O's premier Royal Blue line.

The class B-6, 0-6-0, a hand-me-down from the parent Pennsylvania Railroad (opposite), was the workhorse of the Union Station steam switcher fleet. This one rolled along track 2 in 1949, past the station's secondary powerhouse, which generated steam, hot water, compressed air, and electricity. The powerhouse—smokestack and all—was spectacularly dynamited into a rubble pile in 1976 during Metro subway construction.

Terminal Company directors authorized a spacious Presidential Suite (right), but they turned penny-wise when the time came to furnish it. Because Presidents James A. Garfield and William McKinley had both been assassinated in railroad stations, Union Station executives wanted a secure, if sparse, place away from crowds.

1908. Machinists' wages rise to thirty-two cents an hour for a ten-hour day.

1909. The terminal defends several lawsuits involving locomotive smoke and vibration in neighborhoods fronting the First Street tunnel.

1910. The board objects to purchasing upholstered furniture for the Presidential Suite. President James McCrea agrees that there should be some place to sit down but prefers that the suite be furnished "like a porch. We can't afford expensive furniture." The board approves the purchase of wicker and rattan for not more than $500. The railroads never did pay much attention to the suite. In 1939 government memoranda flew over the sorry state of the room where the British royal couple would be welcomed to Washington. Edward Bruce of the Treasury Department's procurement division wrote President Roosevelt that the suite "is very dingy with all the paint flaking off." The president approved spending $16,000 to paint the suite, cover "unsightly radiators," and replace "cheap-looking wicker."

1912. The Anti-Saloon League claims that women and minors must pass the luncheonette bar, and that it is left unlocked on Sundays; the board approves the purchase of a wire enclosure. A megaphone system of train announcements is tested and found difficult to hear.

1913. At the death of the Terminal Company president McCrea, a flag to drape in mourning is borrowed from the Capitol. The chairman suggests that "it might be well for the Terminal Company to buy a flag for such purposes," but, true to McCrea's parsimony, no action is taken.

1914. The board hears complaints that congressmen, diplomats, and reporters are given the run of station platforms, but others without tickets are not permitted to see off friends and loved ones. The board approves unlimited access to platforms for a ten-cent fee.

1915. Placing benches in the Concourse is considered. The superintendent suggests deferring the project until spring, as "very few people would care to sit in the Concourse during the winter weather."

1926. Board member H. W. Miller of the Southern Railway "had recently experienced some annoyance when going north through Washington at night and again upon his return, by reason of loud talking in the station yards." The board assigns a patrolman to "subdue noise in the vicinity of sleepers."

1931. Depression-era requests for rent reductions from the barber shop, bootblack, Savarin Restaurant, florist shop, and Western Union Telegraph Company are begrudgingly granted. Entire meetings are devoted to "economies of operation."

1936. Following complaints from the U.S. Commission of Fine Arts "relative to the grime which has blackened the statues and architecture of the station," the board orders cleaning of "the more noticeable features."

1941. The board gets no response from the Fine Arts Commission on a proposal to install a marquee in front of the station. The signboard was later approved as an information service to wartime crowds but then ordered down at war's end.

In the 1920s, when the streetcar fare was a nickel, one streetcar pushed off from Union Station to Georgetown via Pennsylvania Avenue (right). The second, like the first owned by the Capital Traction Company, had Connecticut Avenue as a destination. The third was an open car of the Washington Railway & Electric Company. One of Washington's most popular streetcar routes stretched from Union Station across town to American University and the Glen Echo amusement park.

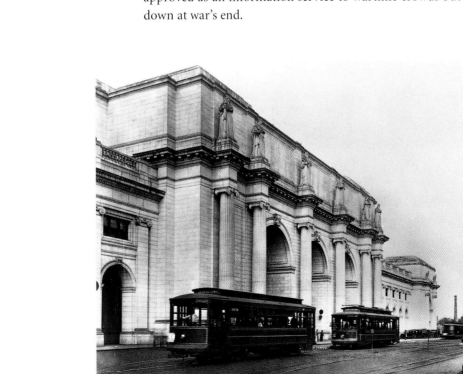

A brief national railroad strike paralyzed the country in 1946. Would-be travelers gazing out from a Concourse gate (left) were indulging in wishful thinking. The strike quickly ended when President Truman threatened to impress striking engineers into the army. By 1973 almost every day was quiet at America's rail-passenger terminals. A Red Cap (below) pushed a baggage cart toward a Metroliner.

1943. Alcoholic beverages are removed from the station drugstore "to cut down on intoxication in trains." Sales would resume four years later "in view of the cessation of hostilities . . . as well as on account of the additional revenue to be derived."

1950. The decline in daily ticket revenue and movement of cars begins to show in board records. From $80,000 and 3,753 cars in 1945, the daily average had dropped to $34,000 and 2,966 cars. By 1963, when the figures were last noted, they would fall below $22,000 and 1,600 cars a day.

1951. As troops again mass at Union Station for trips to Korean War marshaling points, the board gives "sympathetic consideration" to a request to install a billboard "for the purpose of displaying messages of spiritual guidance" but turns it down as "an undesirable precedent."

1952. The notion of appointing a public relations person is rejected, the board believing that the Terminal Company "enjoys excellent public relations" already.

1956. Severe cost-cutting measures include replacing cloth towels with electric hand dryers, installing parking meters, supplanting several Red Caps with luggage carts, closing the employees' Ivy City lunchroom, and eliminating brakemen from many crews.

1964. The station's soda fountain is "retired," replaced by soft-drink machines.

1975. Board minutes grow scant. It is noted that construction of the National Visitor Center is suspended because of a strike.

1978. The terminal manager notifies the board that the National Visitor Center has shut more than half the Concourse, closed numerous offices, and evicted the terminal YMCA "in order to save on the cost of heat."

1981. The board is informed that "all Department of the Interior employees have left [the remnants of the Visitor Center] . . . except for two or three people."

There would be little else beyond auditing reports before the terminal was transferred to a new nonprofit corporation charged with resuscitating the grande dame of rail transportation.

75

In 1965 a worker put the finishing touches on two freshly repainted golden eagles (above), soon to be hoisted atop the flagstaffs in Columbus Plaza—there are three: one for each of Columbus's ships. The hardy crews, working in the snow, would be careful to align the gilded birds properly, because when the set of three eagles was first mounted, someone mistakenly faced one to the east rather than south toward the Capitol.

When it welcomed its first travelers in 1907, Union Station's 760-foot Concourse (opposite), which was open to train platforms, was the largest room in the world. The B&O's Royal Limited listed on the signboard was one of its premier Royal Blue trains. A baggage porter (right) posed to look as if he were rattling down a platform—soon paved with cement—on a battery-powered electric baggage cart. Steamer trunks were common: salesmen traveled with samples, and well-heeled passengers began a transatlantic cruise with a train ride to New York or Baltimore.

EVEN IN THRIVING TIMES, MOST WASHINGTON TERMINAL COMPANY EMPLOYEES WERE INVISIBLE TO THE PUBLIC. THEY HELD MUSCLE POWER "BULL JOBS" IN THE BASEMENT BAGGAGE ROOM, LOCOMOTIVE SHOP, OR COACH REPAIR YARD. IN 1988 FIVE MEN WHO AVERAGED FORTY-SEVEN YEARS IN SUCH JOBS SPUN MEMORIES ABOUT WORKING AT THE STATION.

77

When Elton Miller, a supervisor, was first hired, "a man told me, 'Never rains on the railroad, and furnish your own work clothes.' That meant, 'You come to work, don't make any diff'rence. We expect you to be here,'" he recounted years later. In addition to the twenty-two daily trains to Philadelphia, the fourteen-coach New York trains, and the eighteen-car Florida Specials, he recalled the "crack trains" to the West: the B&O's Capitol Limited and Pennsy's Liberty Limited. Both left each afternoon at 5:30. "When they got to New York Avenue, one would go that way, one would go t'other," Miller said. "It was like the engineers'd race each other coming out."

Shoulder-high sacks, tagged "working mail," were tossed onto each train. "Clerks'd sort it on the way, county by county," Miller said. "They'd make up bags and drop 'em, and mail catchers'd pick up more at each stop." The yards would be full of sleeper cars. "The first one pulled in here, three o'clock in the morning," Miller remembered. "We'd pull 'em off and set them on their own track. People would sleep in the station [yard] all night long. One track was ten, fifteen Pullman cars from different trains." The ritual worked in reverse each evening. "We called it 'nightlining.' You'd get on the train at 8:30 at night and go on to bed. The trains left at two in the morning."

The railroaders loved the old steam locomotives. "Them engineers'd wear a kerchief, goggles on, pants tied at the bottom," said Miller. They had their own living quarters in the engine house, cooked their own meals on an old stone stove. To see ahead, engineers had to stick their heads out the window. "They'd come out the other end of the tunnel, black with soot, and keep right on goin'." Machinist Frank DiMeglio said of the steam engineers, "They'd come out four hours before startin' time, polishing the railings, the bells, oilin' somethin'." To the terminal bulls, engineers were all "Cap": "How you doin', Cap?"

Each engine had a personality. Mechanics could tell which engineer was running which locomotive by the engine and steam whistle sounds: "You could tell it was number 34, and Old Man Brown was running it." The clattering engines kept a huge crew busy at the Ivy City turntable—the spokes of tracks in the maintenance roundhouse. "Every hun'erd miles or so, they'd shake themselves loose: bolts, nuts, fittings," DiMeglio recalled. "Steam engine'd go through those mountains, chuggin' and bouncin' and a-slappin', the bushings'd burn up."

DiMeglio weighed 115 pounds when he started. "Big boilermakers, big rawboned rascals, they'd boot you around," he said. Foremen were the law in the yards. "If you talked to 'em, it was 'Yes, sir,' 'No, sir.' You wouldn't dare suggest anything. You were late? You were gone; they'd fill that job on the spot. Hell, one man would control three hundred trains goin' out. You had to admire 'em. Now, hell, I don't see nothing *but* foremans." Elton Miller remembered a foreman named "Big Ed." "He'd walk through the round-house, people'd scatter." If a mechanic messed up a repair job, he'd sneak out back, bury the part, and start over: better that than face the foreman. DiMeglio said new hires quickly learned the ropes, or else. "I 'member a machinist told me one time, 'Go get an Old Man.' I went out there and got the old man from the toolroom. He said, 'Goddamn it. That ain't the Old Man.' There's a jig you bolt down to drill some holes. *That* was the Old Man."

Three Union Station switching engines pulled cars to the coach yard for cleaning or to the Ivy City car shop for repairs. The pristine condition of the tracks and manicure of the ballast in this photograph give away the era: very soon after Union Station opened.

The general foreman Vincent J. Tana started as a car cleaner. "Water'd freeze right on ya," he said, "but you kept goin'. You were grateful for the job. We'd take firebuckets and barrels, put packin' in 'em [and set them on fire] to keep warm. My paycheck for two weeks, seven days a week, averaged $55. I thought I was a millionaire." Tana would sometimes assist a pipefitter, repairing plumbing at the Savarin Restaurant. "Course I couldn't afford to go in there. Meal'd run ya six bucks. It was outta my league. The chef'd slip ya a chicken leg or somethin'. That was high livin'."

The men remembered Christmases: mail pouches stacked high in Concourse corners, the Main Hall so crowded that "you'd trip over somebody just stretchin' to hear the carols." Said Tana, "Bill Norman, one of the supervisors, 'd play the organ. Ever'body was in a fine mood." Trains would run in two or three sections, each with its own flag whipping past K tower. Passengers arrived two or three hours early to be sure of a seat.

Lawrence Heffner, a foreman, recalled that "ever'body had their own [yard] whistles. They'd want somebody, they'd blow his whistle." The Pennsylvania and B&O had distinctive calls. Terminal Company foremen had theirs, usually two longs and a short, and there was the universal "trouble whistle." When workers heard it, everything stopped. On New Year's Eve at midnight, every whistle in the yard, and on every train, would sound. "You could hear 'em five miles away," said Tana.

Presidential inaugurations were busy, festive times at Union Station. The Erie Railroad, which did not normally run to Washington, in 1921 sent a train pulled by a Pacific-class 4-6-2 for the swearing in of Warren G. Harding, an Ohio native (below). The engine had four pilot wheels, six drive wheels, and two trailing wheels.

Working the "wreck trains" that would sally as far as Brunswick, Maryland, pleased Jim Snyder, a carman. And he loved the company's sports: bowling, playing pool, watching fighters train at the terminal YMCA gym. "We had a ball league, strictly railroad. We'd play at Twenty-first and Constitution Avenue. One time I slid into third, looked up, and there's President Truman, noddin' his head, FBI men about a block away. He wouldn't walk with 'em. I nodded my head, he nodded his and went on down the road."

The men worked on the Ferdinand Magellan, the bulletproof Presidential private rail car. They built a special lift for the crippled F. D. R., replaced bathroom windows an inch thick, cleaned and draped the train for Dwight D. Eisenhower's funeral ("Sure that wasn't *Lincoln's* funeral, Vince?" Heffner cackled), gussied up Mrs. Johnson's Lady Bird Special. They remembered laying the red carpet alongside track 18, down which John F. Kennedy walked to greet King Hassan of Morocco at his rococo private car. But Harry Truman was their favorite. Recalled Tana, "His daughter, Margaret, would go up to New York to take music lessons, and she'd always come back Friday night. Either Harry or Bess or both of 'em'd be there at the station, waiting for train 175. Mr. Truman'd look at his watch and tell me, 'Son, that train's runnin' a little late.' 'Yup,' I'd say. Here he was, the president, and he and Bess'd be out there every week to meet her."

There were lavish private cars: Anheuser Busch's number 10,000, the Adolphus; U.S. Steel Company's stainless-steel-top, red-bottom Fairless; President Roosevelt's first car, the Savannah; the Southern's fleet, brought up for Terminal Company board meetings. And there were the "specials": hundreds of trains for each inauguration, school excursions from West Palm Beach, Democratic and Republican caravans to the spas in Greenbrier, West Virginia, twenty-five trains to the Army-Navy football game in Philadelphia, and, as late as the 1980s, a seven-car White Snake Special for a rock group, arranged by the MTV cable network.

The railroad men warmly recalled the heyday of the railroads: platforms full of kazoo-tooting Shriners, pork dinners with the chef on dining cars, a fresh bass cooked at Seaboard Air Line's own diner out back. (The Seaboard Air Line was a railroad, a predecessor of the Seaboard Coast Line.) But there were lean times, too. During the Great Depression, recalled Frank DiMeglio, "We'd get about eighty-six cent an hour, minus ten percent. They'd take that out for the Terminal Comp'ny, to keep it goin'. You'd work 365 days a year. Take a couple days off, they'd fire you." During the decline of passenger railroads in the 1960s, Lawrence Heffner remembered, "Them New Haven cars'd come in with broke windows. They'd put on a sign, 'vandalism.' But that don't fix the glass. We'd just send 'em back out like they was."

Mostly, though, the work was honest, satisfying. Said DiMeglio, "We'd really roll them engines out."

The work of the "bull gangs" in the train yards was hard and modestly rewarded, but this car repairman, or "car knocker" (above), was probably thankful for it. The work included everything from hefting ponderous cars off their wheels to loading thirty to forty huge blocks of ice into compartments under each coach.

81

## "RUN FOR YOUR LIVES!"

T HURSDAY, JANUARY 15, 1953, HAD DAWNED CLOUDY AND UNSEASONABLY MILD AS TRAIN 173, THE PENNSYLVANIA RAILROAD'S CRACK FEDERAL EXPRESS, GOBBLED ITS LAST TASTE OF SPEED. CHURNING EIGHTEEN MINUTES LATE AND CLIPPING EIGHTY MILES PER HOUR ON THE OWL RUN FROM BOSTON, PENNSY'S GG-1 ELECTRIC ENGINE 4876 AND SIXTEEN SILVER COACHES POUNDED ONTO THE FIRST SWITCHING TRACKS INTO WASHINGTON AT LANDOVER, MARYLAND, TWO MILES FROM UNION STATION.

83

The runaway Federal Express was already out of control as it passed C tower, shown many years earlier. C tower controlled switches near New York Avenue, about half a mile out. It was clear as the Federal roared past K tower, ahead and out of sight in this photograph, that a catastrophe was inevitable. The terminal is visible, peeking above the cross panel and below the Capitol, just ahead. Tracks would have been loaded that mid-January morning in 1953, and controllers had no chance to shunt the runaway onto a siding.

The streamliner's manifest listed four hundred or so coach and sleeping-car passengers, including an early wave of Republican celebrants come to see General Dwight D. Eisenhower inaugurated in five days. Many passengers had already heaved down their bags and were sidling toward the front of the train for a quick getaway at the gate.

Passing Landover, the sixty-six-year-old engineer Henry W. Brower tugged firmly on the air-brake lever. It was an autonomic routine he had performed thousands of times over a long railroading career. The 1,200-ton juggernaut shuddered and reined effortlessly to sixty miles per hour, then, less than a mile later after another nudge, down to fifty.

It was 8:30 A.M.—six minutes to disaster.

At the Ninth Street overpass, Brower again coaxed the brake. This time, the train hiccupped but did not slow down. Adrenaline instantly coursing, the engineer wasted no time pondering. He rammed the brake to "full emergency" for what should have been a squealing panic stop well short of the terminal.

The Federal never paused. It was time to sound the trainman's desperate, staccato "Runaway!" call. Whistle shrieking, the train cannonballed past C tower and then K tower, where the signalman John Feeney had routinely aligned track 16 for its arrival. Stunned to see the train run amok, Feeney frantically considered shunting 173 onto spur tracks. But these were still flush times; adjacent tracks were full.

Too late, anyway. Four city blocks from the terminal and doing forty, the Federal barreled into the one-degree decline toward the station. Feeney grabbed the direct line to the stationmaster's office. "Runaway on 16!" he shouted to the clerk Ray Klopp, who blanched to see the Federal "not more than three or four car lengths" away and bearing down. Klopp leaped from his chair, scattering clipboards, and screamed to four other clerks, "Run for your lives!"

Aboard, passengers formed a freeze-frame of terror. Some clutched the closest soft object: a pillow, a laundry bag, or each other. As the express charged past the Ivy City roundhouse, a woman screamed. T. J. Murphy, the conductor, bounced from car to car. "Get down on the floor! Lie down in your seat!" he hollered.

Dead ahead, frantic alarms had cleared the Concourse. As the monster locomotive slammed into track 16's end bumper, obliterating it, the station clerk Klopp was reaching to dial the rescue services that would surely be needed. After annihilating the rear platform, the engine reared upward like an enraged mustang, burst with a shower of sparks and dust through the stationmaster's shed and station wall, and flopped into the Concourse. The runaway pulverized a concrete stanchion and what an instant before had been the newly expanded Union News Company stand. "I thought somebody had tossed a bomb at one of the trains," said Senator Herman Walker of Idaho, on hand to greet his state's former governor.

It was 8:36 A.M. The time is known because the stationmaster's clock was found crumpled and welded to that moment.

On impact with the end-block bumper, the Federal Express's electric engine reared upward atop debris as it burst through the stationmaster's shed, its collapsible pantograph driving a hole in the Concourse's false ceiling. The engine flopped onto the floor, which gave way near the rear. Had the floor been able to support 230 tons, train 173 might well have pulverized its way into the waiting room. Runaway trains were not unknown within the Union Station yards, although usually it was a slow-moving steam switcher that got away.

Wreckmaster Frank Swofford (right) looked down on the devastation wrought by train 173. The men below were clearing away bits of refuse and looking for spots to attach a crane. "Big Liz," a powerful steam crane now in the B&O museum in Baltimore, had already removed the first coach, which had zigzagged alongside the engine during impact. "Big Liz" flipped the monster electric engine onto its side, and, after a temporary floor was built to conceal the wreck, crews cut the GG-1 into pieces before removing it. Gangs labored in sixteen-hour shifts for three days to clear the debris and ready the station for visitors to Dwight D. Eisenhower's inauguration.

With a bellow, the thick concrete floor collapsed under the engine's 230 tons of deadweight, and engine 4876 and two lead coaches zigzagged into the basement. Four workers in the mammoth baggage room there were trapped briefly, but all survived. Dozens of baggage and mail workers would normally have been posted directly below the 8,000-square-foot crater torn by the falling behemoth. Instead, they were on a fortuitous coffee break.

The third coach settled on a cant at the lip of the hideous hole. Four other cars derailed just outside. Nearby Pennsy employees, Traveler's Aid nurses, and ordinary citizens quickly jumped, or smashed their way, aboard the train to search out the injured. A passenger shattered the smoking-car window with a chair. "I've always wanted to do that!" he exclaimed. There was no fire, just the sizzle of severed brake lines and downed wires.

Somehow, no one was killed; only forty-three persons required hospitalization. Girded to pry out mangled bodies, rescuers instead found none. The engineer and brakeman were led, dazed, from their cab. Neither said a word. Hours later, a newsstand employee was found in a restroom, in shock.

The Concourse was soon a maelstrom of red lights, stretchers, and ambulances. Raymond Klopp and other trainmen got busy heeding the call to "get all the morphine you can" from Union Station's drugstore. D.C. Fire Department pumpers not already fighting another fire, at a tire shop ten blocks away, burst straight into the Concourse and trained their hoses on the crippled engine below. But the GG-1's batteries did not explode; its spilled transformer oil did not ignite.

Thirty-four years later, in retirement in Rockville, Maryland, passenger Edward K. "Bud" Koch flashed back to the horror "like it just happened." He had been inbound from his home in Baltimore to his job as a design artist. As a regular, Koch knew the ordinary, lulling sounds of a comfortably decelerating train. "I realized we had trouble when we hit a switch at what seemed like left angles," he recalled. "We were doin' forty at least, and we weren't slowing down. Joe [a crew member] came runnin' through, told us to brace ourselves. Some people were screaming, but mostly there wasn't time to do much reacting.

"It's funny, but I don't remember much of a noise when it hit. Screeching metal, but no big 'boom.' What I remember was the cloud of concrete dust. That train just tore through the platform like butter, literally powdered it. I ended up on the floor, but I remember seeing something out the window that I'll never forget. In the middle of the dust and the sparks from the electric wires that had been knocked down, I watched, just like it was in slow motion: the undercarriage of one of the cars flew up in the air and came down right next to our car. I don't know to this day how no one was killed."

Reports of the calamity spread quickly. But inquisitive locals and inaugural visitors, including thirty-two full-blooded Arizona Indians in feathered headwear, were surprised, and maybe disappointed, to arrive and find the wreck ingeniously camouflaged within two days of the crash. The shredded stationmaster's office and newsstand were replaced in a whisk, the gaping Concourse hole repaved, even the mangled iron grillwork at the point of entry replaced and freshly painted. Using four hundred workers around the clock, "We had the job licked in thirty-six hours," said the terminal manager Sidney Kerl. Track 16 was back in service within three days.

Even as, a mile away, Ike was swearing to uphold the Constitution as president, the Washington Terminal wreckmaster Frank Swofford's crews were cutting what was left of the $750,000 engine into six giant hunks. News accounts stated that engine 4876 had been sold for scrap, its dials and wires cannibalized. Not so. On orders of Pennsy's insurer, Lloyd's of London, the GG-1 was hauled to the company's Altoona, Pennsylvania, shops, nimbly reassembled, and returned to service. Amtrak later sold 4876 to a New Jersey commuter line, for which it ran until it was mothballed in 1979.

An Interstate Commerce Commission inquiry, convened nine days after the wreck, absolved the train crew; indeed, their bravery was commended. Discounting whispers of sabotage, the commission laid the accident to a frozen angle cock valve in the third coach's air-brake system.

Bud Koch, who had been riding directly above the faulty valve, would be forced to wear a back brace and girdle for more than a year. "I was a bit of a celebrity," he said. "For a long time, people on the train from Baltimore would joke whether, this time, it was going to stop. One fellow laughed and said, 'If they're gonna go *through* the station, they might as well keep on goin' and take me to work.'

"I didn't think it was too funny at the time."

Track 16, along which the runaway had sped, was back in service within three days (below). This Pennsy locomotive had no difficulty stopping well short of the terminal that day, although a car inspector looks as if he was not altogether convinced that the new end-block was secure.

## PART FIVE

At night the station's Massachusetts Avenue arcade took on a ghostly mien (opposite). The building facade is granite, but moving west the materials under the arcade switch from granite to cheaper terra cotta and then plaster. Either the parsimonious railroads put a clamp on Daniel Burnham's budget in midconstruction, or it was agreed going in that the president— whose suite was on the east end—would get granite and the masses could make do with lesser materials. In the late 1940s (right), crews were called out to clear some of the grime that automobiles, steam locomotives, and the passage of time had wrought. The second stone figure, Electricity, has been turned much brighter than its blackened neighbor, Fire.

I N 1948 AMERICANS LOGGED FORTY-FOUR MILLION PASSENGER MILES ON TRAINS AND AIRPLANES. EIGHTY PERCENT TOOK THE TRAIN. NINETEEN YEARS LATER, THE RATIO HAD MORE THAN REVERSED: EIGHTY-EIGHT PERCENT PREFERRED TO FLY. ACROSS THE LANDSCAPE, WORK CREWS LAID RUNWAYS AND WIDE, FAST HIGHWAYS. RAILROADS, FOR WHOM PASSENGER SERVICE HAD BEEN A BREAK-EVEN PROPOSITION AT BEST, PRUNED ROLLING STOCK, SLASHED SCHEDULES, AND GUTTED OR LEVELED SEPULCHRAL STATIONS.

Southern Railway's chief executive officer, Graham Claytor, oversaw that line's reduction of passenger service. Freight business was far more profitable for railroads than the dwindling passenger service, and the prospect of maintaining passenger stations created a financial burden. Later, as Amtrak's president, he noted, "If you're in the freight railroad business, why . . . do you want a mausoleum for a passenger station? All it does is cause trouble, so you get rid of it, quick as you can."

As they retrenched, railroads cried foul about their tax disadvantages. Noted *Railway Age* in 1951, "Union Station in Washington, D.C. . . . cost the railroads $21 million back in 1907; on it, they pay, in addition to all operating expenses and interest, about $290,000 per year in property taxes. . . . By contrast, the railroads' air line competitors use a tax-free Washington airport built entirely at government expense, [and] yet the air lines pay only nominal charges of a few thousand dollars a year for its use."

As late as 1961, when the architectural historian Frederick Gutheim was calling business at Union Station "a ghost of its former self," the terminal was the highest-taxed commercial structure in Washington. Union Station "is a lonely place these days," rued Gutheim. Contemporaries called it "a quiet catacomb" and a "depressing cavern where people no longer come," looked upon by the railroads as "a costly nuisance to be treated with neglect."

The B&O and Pennsylvania Railroads had talked about giving away Union Station even in 1958. But the railroads had a fallback position. They were quietly costing out plans to tear down the monolithic station and throw up an office building. Seymour Auerbach, an architect who conducted such a study, remembered many years later that it was clear that the terminal could not continue as a full-fledged train station. "The railroads had a developer in New York City ready to go," remembered Knox Banner, who headed a business group, Downtown Progress, that as early as 1963 proposed turning Burnham's mighty structure into a visitor and student center. One scheme for a national cultural center—what would become the Kennedy Center for the Performing Arts—suggested turning Union Station into a concert hall. In 1965 a Smithsonian Institution study concluded that Union Station would make a fine railroad museum. But Smithsonian Secretary S. Dillon Ripley passed, noting that other projects, especially an air and space museum, took priority.

But it would not be so easy for the railroads to raze Union Station to build an office tower, as the Pennsylvania Railroad did its storied New York station in 1966. Although the preservation movement was just coming into its own, a quasi-official committee chaired by the Washington architect Francis Lethbridge had, two years earlier, declared Union Station one of twenty buildings in Washington deserving of "category one" landmark status, meaning that "it must be preserved." The designation packed no force whatsoever, other than intense suasion on owners doing business a cinder's throw from Congress. Still, it was clear that something had to be done soon.

An exuberant gathering (opposite) welcomed home the Washington Senators from a successful western trip in which the Nats won nine of ten games in May 1949. The giddy swing moved the Senators into the rarefied first division of the American League. "We can do it," a sign proclaimed, but the team quickly reverted to form, finishing last with a 50–104 record. One train ticket holder in the 1960s must have been both frugal and fussy (below). Scrawlings on the complete voucher show $1.70 later refunded from the $174.57 round-trip double fare.

93

As soon as passenger-rail traffic dropped off, the notion that Daniel Burnham's museum piece might make a dandy visitor center gained momentum. The National Park Service, which had long sought a showcase for tourists, calculated that ten thousand visitors descended on Washington each day, and members of Congress heard the yowls after their constituents scrambled for the Mall's few parking spaces, only to run afoul of zealous meter readers and gypsy tow trucks.

Although it was far from the tourist action of the Mall, Union Station seemed a logical place for an orientation center. It sat at the throat of a likely through-city superhighway—who could know then that only a stub of a road would ever be built? Union Station was set to get one of the city's first subway stops, had plenty of space above its train tracks to park buses and cars, and seemed an ideal spot to store and dispatch "interpretive shuttle" jitneys called tourmobiles. In 1965 Federal Aviation Administrator Najeeb Halaby even suggested that the site could accommodate helicopters and short-takeoff, steep-climbing air-shuttle jets to New York, barreling down a runway paved over the railway marshalling yards. Although that idea never took wing, the notion of turning the old station into a multimodal transportation complex became central to several plans. After all, one of the city's most popular streetcar lines had traversed the city from Union Station to American University and the Glen Echo amusement park in Maryland.

A starry vision crystallized in 1967 when John W. Macy Jr., chairman of the U.S. Civil Service Commission, foresaw Union Station as a locus of America's approaching Bicentennial, "monumental enough to meet the needs of what will certainly be a gigantic birthday party that will attract millions of guests." For the party, Macy even proposed moving "our sacred documents" into the building.

Interior Secretary Stewart L. Udall was a believer. He wrote Macy that the center should indeed be planned on a "grand scale." As Charles Horsky, then adviser to President Johnson for District of Columbia affairs, remembered, "In the guise of seeing whether Union Station could be a railroad museum, we managed to put together a study commission to show it could be a visitors center." The committee report quoted Vice President Hubert Humphrey as taking up the cudgel for tourists: "The time passed generations ago for us in Washington to meet our common obligations to common courtesy."

Inconveniences to passengers that were "deeply regretted" as Union Station was converted into the National Visitor Center in 1976 were nothing compared to the Department of the Interior's later regrets at having begun the center at all. Later passengers would be directed along twisted paths toward a distant train. This cozy Christmastime tableau would be the last good cheer at Union Station for many years. A huge pit soon occupied much of the floor.

94

For the Nation's Bicentennial observance historic Union Station is being converted to the National Visitor Center...

"Any inconvenience caused the traveling public during this conversion is deeply regretted"

Ronald H. Walker
Director, National Park Service

Rogers C.B. Morton
Secretary of the Interior

National VISITOR CENTER

There would be no turning back from plans to tear out the floor of the Main Hall, in preparation for "the Pit" (right). In railroading's heyday, the basement area to the right housed lockers for Terminal Company workers, a few of whom were known to supplement their brawny jobs with a pad-and-pencil sideline: writing the numbers. The basement floor seen here lay close to ground level on the original "Swampoodle" site. Burnham and Company built it up with tons of fill dirt.

Representative Kenneth J. Gray of downstate Illinois chaired the House Subcommittee on Public Buildings and Grounds, and he helped work out a deal that, he would become infamous for saying, "won't cost the taxpayers a penny." Under the 1968 agreement, Union Station's railroad owners would borrow $16 million to reconfigure the building as a visitor center: $5 million for renovation and $11 million to construct a five-level parking structure behind the old Concourse. New York banks would lend the railroads the $16 million because they held exceptional collateral—not only a solid piece of real estate but also a twenty-five-year government lease of the property, at $3.5 million a year. Uncle Sam, in turn, figured to get its money back (and then some) from parking and concession revenues at the new National Visitor Center. And in 2001 for one dollar and payment of any back District of Columbia taxes, the government would have the option of buying Burnham's historic edifice.

In 1973 when Interior Department officials were making one of several trips to Capitol Hill in search of supplemental funding, consultant Barry Howard would describe the National Visitor Center as the "foyer of Washington," ready to serve 5,600 or more visitors an hour. National Park Service guides ultimately counted themselves lucky if two hundred visitors stopped in. As Joe Jensen, a Park Service veteran brought to the project when it got in trouble, would later reflect, "We learned that all roads lead to Rome, but it doesn't necessarily mean that all the *people* go to Rome."

A highlight of tourists' trek through the National Visitor Center was supposed to be a multiscreen slide show, recessed in the Main Hall floor. It was designed, managers told the Senate, "to give people a feeling in their throats and in their hearts that Washington philosophically and physically is the center of our nation." But the hole gouged out for this audiovisual experience in the terrazzo floor, which had replaced the original marble flooring, would soon be immortalized by a less-flattering sobriquet: "the Pit."

The architect Seymour Auerbach related in 1988 that his original plan aimed to avoid cluttering the Main Hall with freestanding exhibits. It called for a glass floor in the basement onto which an orientation map would be projected, visible from that level or from the edges of the breach in the floor above. Light bursts would show the tourmobile route and popular Washington attractions. The Auerbach plan also called for ticket centers and information booths on the basement level, reached by escalators. Ultimately, the National Park Service ran short of funds and cut back the original plan. Even scaled down, the presentation in "the Pit" cost an estimated $1.5 million to design, build, and operate. Auerbach was replaced and the project struggled forward, but the fragments left from the original plan left little hope for success. All that remained was a slide show and escalators that Auerbach called "a route to nowhere."

At first the railroads did little to get the National Visitor Center refitted. They did spend $3.5 million of their own money to build a small replacement depot under the garage skeleton in back, to handle what everyone thought would be the crumbs of passenger service. But in the meantime, the Penn Central, successor to the Pennsylvania Railroad as a half owner of the Terminal Company, had gone bankrupt. Then the highest inflation in memory hit the nation. Remembered former Penn Central Board Chairman Robert W. Blanchette in 1988, "We kept saying, every day, 'The garage has to lose a few hundred spaces.'" When the Interior Department went to the Senate seeking $8.7 million to finally get construction under way in 1973, the projected garage had shrunk from 4,000 to 2,500 spaces.

Temporary wooden flooring (below) gave passengers a reasonably direct route to trains at the tiny Amtrak replacement station that was built out back. Saint-Gaudens's statues might have been turning their backs on the debacle.

97

The multiscreen slide show in "the Pit" was called the Primary Audio-Visual Experience. Several carpeted levels, including the one at the bottom of the far escalator, all led to the same closed-in audiovisual experience. Critics, who were legion, hastily pointed out that Washington's sights could better be seen in person by merely walking out the center's front door.

But there was no turning back. The department was under White House pressure to get something done. In his Bicentennial proclamation, President Richard Nixon had called the visitor center "indispensible." At the same time the Chesapeake & Ohio, which had absorbed the B&O, was realizing the impossible task of refurbishing the station without financial support from the government. Recalls Richard R. Hite, then Interior's comptroller, "So we went to Congress, and we did get $8.7 million in federal funds. That's where we, as a federal entity, got involved with the railroads and their contractor, who were supposed to do the job."

According to George B. Hartzog, director of the National Park Service under Stewart Udall, this was the point at which the visitor center plan began to sour. "I negotiated that contract, so I know what was in it. We weren't going to pay them any . . . rent until they put it in condition. . . . [Rogers] Morton [then Interior Department secretary] and Dick Bodman [his assistant secretary] amended the contract and agreed to pay the railroads rent, at which point [the railroads] said, 'We got a good deal. We get rent, and we don't have to spend any more money.' Why would [the railroads] want to spend another $10 million to put Union Station in shape when you're already getting $3 million in rent [from the Interior Department] without doing anything?"

They did get the thing done, after a fashion. Said Hite of the opening ceremonies on July 4, 1976, "We had a big celebration. We literally could not bring in the Marine Band because we were told the roof would fall in from the reverberation." The Main Hall was covered by a cocoa rug, into which $20,000 in cigarette holes would be burned at one inaugural ball alone five years later.

The National Visitor Center never got auto or bus parking, as it would have cost $4 million more to finish the garage. The city's Metro opened a Union Station–National Visitor Center subway stop, but the line at that time reached only four other close-in locations. Despite a promise of a "tremendous publicity campaign," few if any signs pointing to the center could be found on the streets or the inbound highways of Virginia and Maryland. "The parking garage was the guts of the project," said Congressman Ken Gray years later, "and it never got built. The Nixon administration failed for a lousy $4 million to finish the garage."

Train passengers alighting at the front door ran a marathon gauntlet to their trains. They lugged grips and griping youngsters around "the Pit" in the Main Hall, through a portico to the old Concourse, past displays, then onto a seventy-foot concrete road across the gap between the Concourse and the replacement station. From that depot, riders of long-haul trains faced another serpentine tramp up or down more corridors, stairs, and escalators. Back inside, the visitor center's National Bookstore and sandwich grill drew few customers. Proprietors of the gift shop stapled plywood over the 1907 marble flooring, destroying it, and painted white the room's natural, tricolor marble columns. Upstairs, where Seymour Auerbach had envisioned a short-stay hotel and day-care center, mushrooms would sprout in empty and moldering offices. The Park Service moved its archives of thousands of photographs to Union Station, only to have to pack them off again when rain cascaded through the building's deteriorating roof.

99

Reviews published before, during, and especially after the National Visitor Center's tenure dripped with scorn. In the once-glorious Main Hall, where mahogany benches had been anchored, Charles Ewing of the *Star-News* found multicolored plastic chairs giving "a garish look to the scene . . . like too much rouge on a ruined face." Others wound their way back to Amtrak's train shed and likened it to "a small-town bus terminal." In 1977 the General Accounting Office inspected the building and reported that it was heading for a major structural collapse unless repairs were made.

The Park Service closed "the Pit" on October 28, 1978, barely two years after opening it; the visitor center remained nominally open. In December 1980, leaks in Union Station's roof became unrelenting. Congress eventually authorized another $11 million to plug them, but the contractor was not explicitly instructed to protect the ceiling underneath as repairs proceeded. With the patchwork one-third completed, what was described as a hundred-year storm inundated the building, sending chunks of plaster crashing to the floor, ruining what volumes remained in the National Bookstore and soaking the carpet. Days later a corroded pipeline burst on the third floor of the west wing, spewing ten thousand more gallons of water and further damaging the structure. After the center's last activity for Ronald Reagan's inauguration in 1981, the Park Service closed the National Visitor Center for good. Train passengers were shunted outside through a plywood maze to the Amtrak depot. They would not step inside historic Union Station again for nearly eight years.

Whereas originally the Interior Department had been dealing with railroads that were all too happy to play down passenger service, in 1971 they came face to face with Amtrak, a fresh and vigorous crusader for passenger travel. Early on, Amtrak sued to, if not get the great terminal back, at least secure a better replacement depot, and it squabbled over the National Park Service's desire to close the visitor center in off-hours to save on utility costs, which would have forced train passengers outside in the dead of night. As the department's luck would have it, a gasoline shortage hit the nation in the winter of 1973–74, and Amtrak's high-speed Metroliners to New York were catching on—just as the Park Service was kicking out the trains. Noted William H. Jones of the *Post*, "Like the Australian aborigines, the American passenger train was thought to be doomed. . . . But like the aborigines, who refused to die out, the passenger train has become increasingly popular."

Each section of damaged plaster (opposite) later had to be chipped away, then recast and replaced. The restoration architects found at least one source of the damage: the station's granite had been stacked in layers, with no caulking, and wind blew water into the joints.

Water, water, everywhere—the result of sievelike leaks in the station roof. Pools formed around columns in the east end of the Concourse, facing the waiting room (above). When the roof was temporarily dissected and repairs undertaken, a hundred-year storm rained through the exposed ceiling and the floors and furnishings below. Cruel critics of the fiasco suggested that the rainwater might be useful in "the Pit"—to convert it into an aquarium.

101

The master restoration specialist John Barianos (above, in the white shirt) and his apprentice Apostolos Papadimitris applied delicate leafing to an eagle in an alcove of the terminal's Presidential Suite. For years the eagle had hovered in faded red, gold, and blue. Barianos followed the dictum of a faithful preservationist—restoring the emblem to Burnham's original white-with-silver-leaf design.

In his Rockville, Maryland, studio (opposite), Barianos cleared away imperfections from a newly cast column capital. Before tackling the monumental Union Station, the family had applied its restorative skills to projects at the White House, Willard Hotel, Treasury Building, and Old Post Office. Helen Barianos, son Vasilios (Bill), and daughter-in-law Irene helped out. The younger generation cast additional capitals to replace ones that were chipped, defaced, or lost outright.

# BACK ON TRACK

HUMAN NATURE DROVE MOST POLITICIANS AND GOVERNMENT BUREAUCRATS MANY ARMS' LENGTHS FROM UNION STATION AFTER IT CLOSED IN 1981. BUT TWO SENATORS, DEMOCRAT DANIEL MOYNIHAN OF NEW YORK AND REPUBLICAN ROBERT STAFFORD OF VERMONT, AND HOUSE PUBLIC WORKS CHAIRMAN JAMES J. HOWARD OF NEW JERSEY STEPPED FORWARD TO CHAMPION UNION STATION ANEW ALMOST FROM THE MOMENT THE NATIONAL VISITOR CENTER CLOSED. "UNLESS WE WANT THE STATION TO BECOME A RUIN, WE MUST DO SOMETHING," MOYNIHAN SAID.

The transformation of "the Pit" back into a real train station began with dismantling the audio-visual theater in the ground (above left). The floor was then rebuilt to accommodate the new marketplace downstairs (above right). Three sets of scaffolding, including one "traveler," were used to restore the Main Hall (opposite left). Finally, a new central kiosk especially for dining took form in the reclaimed space (opposite right).

First, Congress approved the roof repairs. Then, when it passed the Redevelopment Act of 1981, the Interior Department was directed to relinquish the building—which it did happily. The Department of Transportation gained the lease and began to fulfill the act's requirements: to redevelop the station as a transportation terminal and, secondarily, as a commercial center; to preserve the building; to return passenger rail service; and to bring in commercial development to support the station financially. Next the Federal Railroad Administration commissioned an engineering survey that eliminated any surprises lurking behind the old walls and a market study showing that specialty retail and office development would be profitable.

"Graham Claytor [president of Amtrak] was looking to beef up Amtrak's image," remembered Robert W. Blanchette, the former Penn Central board chairman and Federal Railroad Administration administrator, "and nothing was worse for its image than that horrible place with mushrooms sprouting from offices. We were assured of support on the Hill; the members of the Senate could look out their windows and see what the federal government had wrought upon an unsuspecting citizenry." Noted Mark Lindsey, chief counsel of the Federal Railroad Administration, "It was to be Amtrak's headquarters station, in sight of the place from whence its subsidy comes. And it's the station more Americans will see than any other, even if they're not riding the train."

The new secretary of transportation enthusiastically embraced the take-over. "Thank God for Elizabeth Dole," said Amtrak's Claytor in 1988. Dole helped find $70 million in Amtrak funds to get the station refurbished. In the meantime Charles Horsky, President Johnson's adviser for District of Columbia affairs, was, as he put it, "conspiring" on behalf of an influential business group, the Federal City Council, with City Administrator Tom Downs. "The District has x million dollars in interstate highway money that we can't spend," Horsky later quoted Downs as saying. "We haven't got any plans for it, and it will revert to the Treasury in about eighteen months if nothing is done. I think that the District would be willing to put in [what turned out to be $40 million] to finish the garage, and if we finish the garage, maybe we can make something happen." In a sense, the parking garage at a city train station thus became part of the interstate highway system.

Horsky and Lindsey drafted the articles of incorporation for a nonprofit Union Station Redevelopment Corporation, to be chaired by Dole. In keeping with the new Reagan administration emphasis on public-private partnership, "We said," remembered Blanchette, "'Let's do a private company as a convincing demonstration that this wasn't going to be on the public dole.'"

The station's old Concourse (pages 106–7), where passengers originally caught their trains, was reshaped into three shopping levels by the Union Station Redevelopment Corporation. The beginnings of a mezzanine are visible, while work proceeded on the main and basement levels. Portions of the roof were cut out and strengthened, and the huge room took on a scrubbed appearance never seen in the dingy, dim-lit days of heavy train travel.

Restoration addressed the terminal's decorative features as well as nitty-gritty details. Wisely secured to a safety belt and rope on his perch forty feet above the Main Hall floor, Romero Chavez (opposite) gave one of Saint-Gaudens's legionnaires a long-overdue bath and facial. Another worker (right) undertook the task of constructing the floor of the new Concourse shopping level.

The redevelopment corporation was authorized to return Union Station to railroad service. The historic Concourse became Amtrak's ticketing and baggage facility as well as the three-level marketplace center. The Main Hall was set aside as a restored space without commercial enterprises. In back of the terminal the District government, using its highway funds, finally completed the parking decks (reduced further to 1,300 auto spaces), and a tour bus level and the Amtrak waiting area were added. The old station's usable space was thus just about doubled, as the original unheated (and uncooled) Concourse had drawn traffic only at train time.

Amtrak rented the building's upstairs offices as its national headquarters, set about demolishing the tiny replacement station, and brought the tracks back flush against its new staging area. Now pleased that the railroads had not done the prudent thing and torn down the terminal thirty years earlier, Claytor would say of "the southern terminus of the Northeast Corridor" in 1988, "It's the finest railroad station in the United States again, without any question. Burnham would be proud of it."

The redevelopment agreement called for a $70 million contribution from Amtrak, with the Federal Railroad Administration assuming yearly lease payments to the railroads (it later exercised an option to buy the station). Selected after a national competition, the marketplace developers—LaSalle Partners, Williams Jackson Ewing, and Benjamin Thompson Associates—agreed to pay a base rent, indexed for inflation, plus a split of the profits to the redevelopment corporation, which in turn was to repay Amtrak from its revenues. The new general contractor, the Dick Corporation, and the construction manager, Gilbane-Smoot, set to work.

Restoration was a painstaking process. Billy Ford, a plaster worker, replaced a damaged capital on one of the Ionic columns in the Presidential Suite (right). Still to come, on the wall to the left, was one of the many gilded, globed fixtures that adorned the fancier rooms in the terminal.

After the project was reviewed by the Advisory Council on Historic Preservation, the U.S. Commission of Fine Arts, the National Capital Planning Commission, and the District's historic preservation officer, the developers agreed to reduce four kiosks in the Main Hall to one and to maintain relatively unobstructed views of the terminal's lofty ceilings. "People may think we've done violence to the Concourse, when we put three levels where only one existed," said Keith Kelly, president of the redevelopment corporation. "But that was not basically a historic structure. It was a train shed." The commercial space would feature a "dining room of particular distinction and appeal" in the old presidential reception room.

In a 1982 editorial supporting modest redevelopment, the *Post* could not resist a sarcastic look back: "Don we now our hip boots and foul-weather gear for another depressing trip into leaky old Union Station, long the unproud home of not much at all except downpours of water and federal dollars and, it is said, a flourishing rat population." Rodents were not the only nuisance found by the first team of preservation architects to enter the building. Advance teams from Harry Weese and Associates encountered pigeons, chicken bones, human excrement, and, according to the project architect Karl Landesz, "bums sleeping down there." Said the field architect Tom Bronson, "You'd stand two blocks away and think you were looking at a monument. Inside, it . . . looked like something that should have been condemned, and it was about to be. It was like a crime had been committed." "Butchery," as they characterized it, from National Visitor Center days included parquet floors buckled three-feet high, plaster "in chunks the size of a small room," and the west lobby ceiling "full of holes like Swiss cheese."

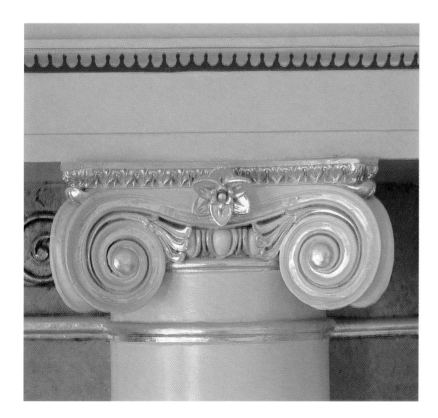

111

After the plasterwork was recreated, a touch of Midas made the classical features glisten. Gold leaf was applied to highlight the spiraling volutes of the capitals as well as details above and below to attract the eye of visitors (left). Restoration specifications called for gold leaf, not just gold paint, and more than seventy pounds of leafing was delicately applied. At gold prices current in the late 1980s, that represented an investment of almost $500,000.

On March 7, 1984, Interior Secretary William P. Clark signed documents formally transferring jurisdiction of the building to the Department of Transportation, and the mixed-use redevelopment was on. Keith Kelly of the Union Station Redevelopment Corporation felt confident that the marketplace project would not fail if the six traffic-flow segments—Amtrak passengers, commuter-rail customers, subway riders (estimated by Metro at fifteen thousand a day at the Union Station stop in 1988), tour-bus visitors, congressional lunchers, and neighborhood residents—all kicked in, and if the terminal did indeed prove to be the taproot of redevelopment across the eastern end of the city's ceremonial core.

"As fast as we possibly could," said Kelly, "we covered 'the Pit.'" A gritty task—turning a sodden, abandoned transportation shrine into a multiuse showplace—fell to the Dick Corporation, whose $48,310,500 bid acceptance by the redevelopment corporation in 1986 set loose a pressure-packed race to meet a deadline for a candlelight reopening gala scarcely two years away.

More than three hundred craftsmen bent to Project Superintendent Gene Butler's direction amid a blur of dust and a caterwauling of saws, mixers, and jackhammers. In the frantic final week in early September 1988, the number would swell to more than eight hundred—European artisans, American journeymen, even sweep-up laborers recruited from Washington halfway houses.

The Dick Corporation's task was prodigious: covering and reshoring "the Pit"; dropping the basement floor five feet to accommodate theaters, cafes, and baggage handling; installing new concealed heating and cooling ductwork. Crews tearing into shafts never before opened unveiled a bonanza of collectibles: 1905 bottles, newspapers, spoons, pepper cans, and even a hand-carved, six-foot propeller that had likely been part of a crude cooling system. The latter-day contractors practically had to redesign as they went, firing off more than a thousand urgent "RFIs"—requests for information—to architects and historical researchers as they poked into crannies never before revealed.

Bush-hammer operators ran into a massive metal deck and concrete slab where the Federal Express had burst through the Concourse floor in 1953. Electricians struggled to trace conduits buried in granite walls. Experts argued whether a shadowy effect in an old black-and-white photograph of the Presidential Suite was a deliberate "leathering look" fashionable at the time or an accident of reflected lighting. The leathering effect won the day, and Dick artisans sponged layers of mottled brown paint and lacquer onto the final canvas.

Project Manager John T. Sebastian supervised this beehive. "In the winter, we had to get heat into the building so the painting, stenciling, canvasing and plastering would take," he noted. "There were no functioning utilities, so we set up boilers on semi-trailers outside that pumped twelve million Btu's into that building."

112

Foreman Paul Levidiopis (above) of the Barianos Company poured a plaster mixture into a mold to recreate original features. When the plaster forms but has not completely dried, a template is pulled across it, creating the pattern to fit the section of ceiling or wall to be restored. Excess plaster is then chipped off so that the molded piece fits snugly.

The restoration moved from floor to ceiling. To restore the main floor pattern, Spyros Xanthos (left) set reddish "Champlain dots" in place in the white marble flooring. The West Hall's glass ceiling (pages 114–15) got a new coat of paint to refresh Burnham's dazzling canopy of light. The architect made sure that sunshine streamed in through skylights and overscaled windows.

A dedicated train buff, the former weather-watcher Willard Scott of NBC's "Today Show" emceed Union Station's gala reopening. Grand pianos tinkled, newsboys in knickers hawked an "extra," pasty-gray human models of Saint-Gaudens's statues posed, and tap dancers decked out as a snaking model train did temporary violence to the new marble floor.

So meticulous would be the restoration that Weese paint consultant Frank Welsh scraped to find the original 1907 colors of walls. "There were twenty-two layers of paint in the Main Hall," said Karl Landesz, the project architect. "Frank took a sharp knife and chipped off a cross section and put it under a microscope, so he could actually read each layer. Once you're down to bare plaster, the first two coats, you figure, are primer, so the third coat out is the original color. But because that color deteriorated over time, he actually scraped *into the middle of that third layer* under the microscope, to match the color using a notation system. Then he could reproduce almost that exact color."

John Barianos, who was charged with restoring everything from Saint-Gaudens's silent sentinels to the intricate Pompeian traceries, went so far as to duplicate Burnham's delicate dying process in creating red-tinted scagliola for the marble columns in the new dining room. Washington horologist Elton Louis Howe was commissioned to restore the large east wall clock and two smaller ones. He found that someone, during a "modernization" effort in the 1940s, had junked the clocks' original Magneta Company workings, clipped out and thrown away internal bulbs, replaced glass covers with plastic, and "worst of all in a Roman building," snapped in clock faces that had arabic numbers. His recreated clocks featured decidedly roman numerals.

Thousands of people thronged Union Station for its grand reopening on September 29, 1988. The building was bedecked with flags and bunting. Washingtonians whose recent experiences at the terminal had been forlorn gaped in astonishment at the incredible transformation.

Few feats of restoration could match, for pure persistence, the saga of the Concourse ceiling glass, half of which had been shattered over time and needed replacing. Don F. Cooper, the senior project manager, held in his hand a square of glass, three-eighths inch thick, etched with Florentine swirls and laced with protective chicken wire: typical safety glass of Burnham's day. Cooper soon determined that it had been crafted by Pittsburgh Plate Glass in 1904, and it seemed simple enough to duplicate for the ten thousand or so square feet of ceiling that needed to be reglazed.

Cooper picked up the tale of what became a maddening Union Station scavenger hunt: "It was a common kind of rolled glass, but PPG quit making it in 1912. You could go down to any hardware store and find wire mesh, but not that fine a pattern, and it would be made of the wrong kind of material. This was a special alloy to which molten glass would adhere. I called every steel manufacturer, told them I'd pay extra money to recreate that process, that I'd buy ten times more than I needed. They said 'No, no way.'

"Then there was that distinctive swirl pattern. We finally found someone who said, 'Yeah, there was a plant down in Louisiana that would roll that kind. 'We went down there, and the plant had been disassembled five years ago; couldn't find any machinery or anybody who might have kept it as a souvenir. We called manufacturers of patterned glass all over the world—Italy, Korea, even a place in India—nothing. We ended up going to an art place in Indiana that makes glass for shower stalls and Tiffany lamps. Somebody there said he got the patterns from a toolmaker in New Jersey. So I trucked up to New Jersey, and we found two or three old people who knew how to roll out a piece of this glass using acid. So we got the roller, the pattern.

"The art-glass place couldn't roll it; it couldn't control the temperature enough to get a consistent pattern. So we went down to Kingsport, Tennessee, to AFG Industries. Twenty-four hours a day, they run patterns for huge national retailers. I practically begged them to run our pattern. They said, 'We shut down for only six hours a *year*.' I explained the Union Station project, really sold its historical value, said they could put the fact that they helped us in their brochure! Finally they relented, and they made the glass we needed.

"But we still didn't have the wire. We tried everywhere, and it just couldn't be done. What we ended up doing was laminating this new, patterned glass to safety glass, to ensure safety. In Kingsport, I noticed that they were putting designs on the glass—literally painting on decorations. I said, 'Why don't we *paint* the wire pattern! We don't need the wire for safety.' We found some little old guy who was willing to give it a try, and it worked. So we virtually created a whole new technology for historical glass. It took a year and a half, and we didn't get the last shipment until a week before grand opening, but the job got done. Now half the [Concourse] ceiling is original glass, half is this new product that took us eighteen months to put together, and you can't tell the difference."

Looking back wistfully, while preparing to leave Washington for another, less-epic assignment, John Sebastian, the project manager, reflected, "Union Station has been a bit like raising a child and having to send it off on its own. It was exhilarating, especially at the grand opening, when people seemed impressed that we'd raised the child correctly. But it's also a hollow feeling, having to move on."

Americans had retained a deep affection for Union Station. Many recalled every detail of shoving off to war there, or falling in love, or just lounging between trains. One man in his thirties, Charles Rich, remembered hurrying as a wide-eyed kindergartner with his brother and father into the station's game room to cut a scratchy, five-inch phonograph record on which to wish Mama Rich *bon voyage*.

Don Cooper, too, waxed philosophic: "Our hope is that, eighty years from now, when people go to restore this building again, they'll be able to come back to the work we did, go through our research and records and patterns that we used to recreate 1907, and have a solid base from which to again perpetuate the inspiration of Daniel Burnham. Like him, maybe we were able to stop time for a moment."

Spectacular fireworks concluded the 1988 reopening festivities. A triumphant example of public-private partnership had been completed on time and on budget. That partnership continued on many levels: the U.S. Department of Transportation retained the land beneath the station; quasi-public Amtrak moved its headquarters there and became an ownership partner; the area's transit authority brought in subway service; and private investors helped finance the project, assumed ownership of the building, and rented space to retailers.

119

Eighty-one years after the first train left Burnham's titanic terminal, work crews pulled away the construction horses and plywood walkways, and the public got its first look inside the station in almost eight years (right). The night before, Washington's *haute monde* crowded the Main Hall for a black-tie, candlelight pre-opening gala for three thousand, complete with mournful train whistles, a light show, and terminal lore.

For many visitors, each glimpse of the revitalized station (left and opposite) brings back a pleasant memory. For the young and the young at heart, Union Station represents a memorable place to shop, eat, and catch a train or a movie. The reopened terminal quickly became a destination, both for local sightseeing services and for out-of-town tour buses, whose passengers use Union Station as a base of operations for visiting the nation's capital.

Union Station's festive food court (opposite) includes more than thirty vendors and seats six hundred. The terminal has turned into a favorite venue for presidential inaugural balls. More than ten thousand people crowded the station in 1997 (above) to toast Bill Clinton. Public exhibits have included a display by Ringling Bros. and Barnum & Bailey Circus (left).

Onetime British Prime Minister Margaret Thatcher celebrated her seventieth birthday at Union Station in 1995 (left). The Main Hall's soaring ceilings and heroic statuary (opposite) never fail to cause first-time visitors to tip back their heads for an admiring look upward. From its carriage way on the left to the presidential entrance on the right (pages 126–127), Union Station emulated the majestic buildings of ancient Rome. A monument to transportation, the grand terminal signaled the arrival of Washington as a world capital.

The author and photographer extend special appreciation to Herbert H. Harwood, former chief commercial administrator of the Chesapeake & Ohio system and interim director of the Baltimore & Ohio train museum in Baltimore, for sharing his considerable expertise on the railroad that formed half of the Washington Terminal Company ownership. Similarly, Robert Emerson, director of the Railroad Museum of Pennsylvania in Strasburg, provided invaluable leads and information on the Pennsylvania Railroad half of terminal history. The superb rail historian John P. Hankey of the University of Delaware graciously shared memorabilia from his collection of railroad mementos and gave the manuscript a sound railroader's inspection before the final "all aboard."

Keith Kelly, the late president of the Union Station Redevelopment Corporation, opened his files and bountiful expertise to make the original book possible in 1988. Stan Bagley, Amtrak's general superintendent in Washington, kindly made both board of directors records and many of his capable staff of veteran train men available, leading to many of the most memorable anecdotes in this volume. All whose reminiscences are recited herein were generous with their time and interest, and we are especially grateful to retired Interior Department executive Richard R. Hite, who helped sort out the confusing and controversial days when Union Station became the National Visitor Center.

Special thanks go, too, to streetcar expert LeRoy O. King Jr.; to veteran Washington Terminal Company engineer (and excellent amateur photographer) William R. Hutson; and to the capable people at the Martin Luther King Library (especially Washingtoniana Division chief Roxanna Deane), the Library of Congress, Imagefinders, and the Historical Society of Washington, D.C., for their assistance in locating historic photographs.

We are grateful to Robert Maurer, director of marketing for LaSalle Partners, and Lisa M. Reliford, special events coordinator, for their support in undertaking this new edition. We also salute Diane Maddex and Robert Wiser of Archetype Press for their editorial and design skills in revising the original book.

*Illustration Credits*

All contemporary color photographs are by Carol M. Highsmith except as indicated below.

Associated Press: 54, 64–65
Pete Copeland, *Washington Star*/D.C. Public Library, Washingtoniana Division: 74 bottom
D.C. Public Library, Washingtoniana Division: 36, 37 bottom, 55, 75, 82–83, 84–85, 86, 87, 92–93, 94–95, 97
Graham, Anderson, Probst and White, Inc., Architects, Chicago: 2, 57 top
Steven Halperson/Tisara, Inc.: 123 both
John P. Hankey Collection: 67, 93
Jack Hartzman/MH Photography: 124
Historical Society of Washington, D.C.: 4, 35, 43 bottom, 46 bottom
William R. Hutson Collection: 71
John F. Kennedy Memorial Library: 66
LeRoy O. King Jr. Collection: 40 bottom, 50–51, 73, 78–79
Kiplinger Washington Editors Collection: 34, 38–39, 42
LaSalle Partners: 49
Library of Congress: 37 top, 39 top, 45 middle and bottom, 46 top, 48, 62
Library of Congress, Dunlap Society Collection: 63
Library of Congress, Prints and Photographs Division: endleaves, 6, 39 bottom, 43 top, 47, 56, 58, 60, 64, 70, 72, 76, 77, 91
National Park Service: 96, 98–99, 101
Pennsylvania Avenue Development Corporation: 44
Smithsonian Institution: 40 top
Smithsonian Museum of American History, Warshaw Collection: 41
Nina Tisara/Tisara, Inc.: 117, 118–19
Union Station Redevelopment Corporation: 45 top, 61
Union Station Venture, Inc.: 8, 59, 74 top, 80, 81
Harry Weese and Associates: 57 bottom

"SO IT IS IN TRAVELLING—
A MAN MUST CARRY
KNOWLEDGE WITH HIM
IF HE WOULD BRING
HOME KNOWLEDGE."

SAMUEL JOHNSON
LETTER, APRIL 17, 1778
QUOTED IN *THE LIFE OF JOHNSON*
(JAMES BOSWELL, 1791)